Call me Mistress

Jessica Black

ACORN BOOKS
www.acornbooks.co.uk

This edition published in 2015 by
Acorn Books
www.acornbooks.co.uk

Acorn Books is an imprint of
Andrews UK Limited
www.andrewsuk.com

Contents

Call me
Mistress

Prologue

It was just another Sunday morning as I showered and changed, I sat down at the kitchen table, took a little coffee and some muesli and afterwards walked the dog through the small copse at the back of the house calling in to the newsagents en route, picking up my usual copy of the Sunday Times.

I don't normally check my emails on a Sunday, sort of a golden rule that although I'm not religious the Sabbath really should be treated as a special day. The lid on my Mac Pro was open and I swept my finger over the mouse pad as it came to life. More in habit than anything else I logged onto the internet, checked out my friends' latest posts on Facebook and clicked onto my Gmail account. I had several new messages, one from a potential new client or so I thought. It was a Hotmail account 'John0057', no surname, a clear indication that he'd set up the account for this purpose only and wanted to remain anonymous.

The email was very detailed, very specific and my mouth fell open as he told me everything he wanted me to do to him and the kind of money he demanded I take from him. Yes you read that right... I was to demand money from him, my slave. He wanted to see me that week, Tuesday afternoon to be specific and even detailed what I had to wear: tight shiny leggings, and a sexy, loose cream silk blouse right down to the Louboutin shoes, he was very specific about those red soled shoes.

At first I thought he was some sort of crank but his email had obviously taken some time and effort and he was talking about paying me silly money and there was no sexual contact. This wasn't possible I thought to myself. Why would any man take sexual gratification being degraded and abused in this way?

I read on; he told me that he had followed me on the many sites I was now registered with. He said Mistress Zeta was everything he'd ever dreamed of and he would be eternally grateful if I deemed him worthy. Finally he told me he lived in Wimbledon which was no more than an hour's drive from where I lived.

I printed off the email and slipped it into my handbag, I'd think about contacting him on Monday perhaps. I read over the email several times that day and as I enjoyed a solitary glass of wine later that night I convinced myself that I'd be a fool not to show up and see if it was too good to be true. I would be in my own car; he would be stood on the pavement waiting for me and if I didn't like the look of him I could always drive away.

I left it until quite late on the Monday and my reply was harsh and to the point. I'd studied the area on Google Maps.

"Be on Havelock Road at ten thirty, near to the Garfield Road Recreation Ground. I will know who you are. I can smell a loser a mile off."

He replied back immediately by iPhone. "Yes Mistress Zeta."

My God, I was panicking now, would he turn up, would I turn up? This was dangerous and of course I wasn't over familiar with the area either. And yet the more I thought about it the more I wanted to give it a try. "Live dangerously, nothing ventured nothing gained!," I reminded myself as I ran upstairs to change.

I turned onto Havelock Road twenty minutes late. It was quiet, the last of the dog walkers long gone and as I passed Havelock Road on the left, sure enough, two hundred metres past the Recreation Ground as the road swept round to the right he was waiting.

I knew it was him as I reduced my speed and crawled slowly past him. For a second he seemed to want to follow the car but I drove on past. I wanted a closer look and anyway it would do no harm to tease him a little. I indicated and turned right onto Plough Lane. I stopped a hundred yards up the road and did a three point turn coming back on myself as I mentally slipped into character.

As I drew towards him I wound down the window to take a closer look. I slowed almost to a stop. It was dark but the car lights picked him out as he bent forward to peer in the window. A businessman, he had that look, early forties, slightly overweight, too many lunches and not enough exercise but no, there was no resemblance to Fred West or Hannibal Lecter and I felt compelled to stop.

"Loser!" I shouted.

"Yes Mistress."

It was him. I took a quick look up the road and checked in my rear view mirror. It was clear and I brought the car to a halt as I reached for the roll of tape on the passenger seat.

"Stay where you are, you pathetic wretch, stay where I can see you," I called out.

"Yes Mistress."

He looked like a nervous wreck as I stepped from the car, he wore a pair of beige chinos and I noticed almost immediately a large bulge in the front of his pants.

"What the hell is that?" I said, pointing to his trousers.

He was stuttering. "Sorry Mistress I have dreamt of this fantasy for so long, it's all too much for me."

I walked a little nearer to him, he almost seemed to back away and I felt in total control as he looked down at the floor like a schoolboy in the headmaster's office. He was snivelling, apologising over and over again as I brought the roll of duct tape up to his nose waving it in front of his face. (He'd specified the tools of the trade in his email and even told me the duct tape had to be silver.)

"Turn around you tosser and put your hands around your back."

"Yes Mistress Zeta."

He did exactly as he was told and I wrapped the tape tightly around his wrists. I was in total control and beginning to enjoy the occasion. I spun him around to face me and moved my right hand down to his groin and squeezed.

"I tell you when to get hard." I sneered at him. "Is that clear?"

"Yes Mistress Zeta."

"I tell you when to get excited and I decide if you come or not. Remember, you are my slave and I am in total control is that clear?"

"Yes Mistress Zeta."

"When I have finished with you I am going to cut your clothes to shreds and take every penny you own. You are a fucking worthless piece of shit do you understand?"

"Yes Mistress Zeta, I love you and I am yours to do as you please."

I opened the rear car door and almost kicked him in. He lay whimpering on the seat as I climbed in and I wondered if this was really happening as I followed his email instructions almost to the letter.

"You're my bitch now, my slave and don't you ever forget it." I said as I started the engine.

"Yes Mistress Zeta."

I turned around and drove in the direction of Wandle Meadow Nature Reserve, there was a small track that cut across the land which would be a little more private and allow me to carry out the final piece of this man's fantasy. I turned left as I located the entrance to the track and drove the car at speed as I found the place I was looking for. It was a popular spot for courting couples but thankfully it appeared to be deserted that night. I climbed out of the car and threw the back door open as I leaned in. "Your wallet loser, where is your wallet?"

"My pocket Mistress," he said excitedly.

I studied the creature that lay sprawled across my back seat. He had that look on his face; you know the type of look I mean? The look a man can't hide when he is aware that sexual release is near. At that point he almost appeared ordinary. This was normality for him, he was experiencing the exact type of sexual sensations a regular guy would experience when watching a porn film for example and at that moment he was fast approaching his climax and as his make believe Mistress I had to guide him on his way and act out his fantasy to the end.

He was lying on his back, his erection clearly visible through his trousers but he had no possible way of relieving himself.

I reached into the back and physically dragged him out of the car as he fell into the dusty earth. His tears were visible now as they streaked his cheeks but this was all part of his fantasy. I knelt down towards him and unbuttoned his flies. His cock almost burst from the gap in his trousers, standing stiffly upwards, proud, swollen and angry looking.

He was shaking his head.

"My wallet," he said, "my wallet."

It was two simple words but they almost blew me away, a surreal moment. Picture the scene, this man was on the point of orgasm and all he wanted me to do was to reach for his wallet and take his money. I knew how much he had offered me in his email and it was a lot of money. I was thinking to myself that surely he would try and demand some sort of physical release now that he had a raging hard on and that would be when I would tell him to take a hike.

But he didn't.

"My wallet," he repeated desperately. "Take my money Mistress, please."

I couldn't quite believe what was happening, couldn't quite get my head around the fact that this man wanted me to relieve him of his money more than anything even at time like this. So I did as he asked and began searching his pockets for a wallet. I found it, a big fat wallet to be precise crammed with twenty and fifty pound notes.

"You miserable cretin," I mocked as I pulled out a fistful of notes. "This is mine do you understand?"

"Yes Mistress Zeta. Take it, take more, take anything you want."

"Who deserves it most?" I asked.

"You do Mistress Zeta."

I did as he asked, three or four times as I emptied his wallet and abused him verbally all the while. I could sense he was nearing his climax as I told him I was leaving him where he lay and he would need to find his own way home. He let out a stifled cry as he climaxed there and then and ejaculated over his trousers and shirt and I continued to abuse him.

"You filthy, dirty, horrible, bastard. I didn't give you permission to do that, you wait until your Mistress gives you permission do you hear?"

"Yes Mistress Zeta, I'm sorry."

I yelled at him again. "You do that the next time without my permission and we are finished do you hear?"

"Yes Mistress Zeta I am so sorry it won't happen again."

It was time for the final piece of the drama and probably the bit that I found the most bizarre. I took the scissors from the glove compartment and cut his clothes to shreds pulling his soiled trousers from around his waist, ripping them from him violently and casting them into some nearby bushes. I took his shoes off too and threw them down the darkened track, but I didn't throw them too far because I wanted him to find them.

Although I was still very much in my wicked Mistress Zeta role I was also me and I couldn't help feeling sorry for the man. I couldn't abandon him like that could I? Surely he'd had his orgasm and the role play had been completed and I could wipe him down and bundle him in the back and drive him back home or to wherever his car was parked?

He must have sensed exactly what I was thinking and for the first and last time he gave me an instruction.

"Leave me, Mistress," he said weakly as he wallowed in his own filth. "Go," he said.

And so I did.

As I drove away watching my newest customer in my rear view mirror, stranded, still with his hands bound behind his back I couldn't help but feel bad for leaving him there and I wondered how the hell he would get loose and where his car was. Different scenarios played out in my head. What if the police found him walking the streets in that state in just a pair of boxers and a spunk stained ripped up shirt? Someone could have taken my number plate and I'd be arrested. My God how would I explain that?

But it had all been on the booking information in the email, I was to leave him there stranded and helpless and above all with no money to get home. So that's what I had done, those were my instructions, my job description, anyhow he wasn't far from a main street so he would be fine, I had made sure of that and comforted myself with that thought.

Twenty minutes later I comforted myself with another thought as I pulled into a 24 hour supermarket car park. I counted up the money I had taken from him. It amounted to exactly a thousand pounds. He'd kept to his word, said that's how much he would pay me if I acted out his fantasy to the letter and I had.

I sat for some minutes wondering if I had imagined everything, was it a dream and was I about to wake up? I stuffed the notes into my handbag and looked in the mirror. I looked good, my make-up still perfectly in place and apart from a little bit of dust on my leggings which I brushed off you'd think I'd just left the house ready for a night out with the girls. I'm not surprised, I'd kept my clothes on throughout what amounted to a forty minute acting performance, no dancing or stripping for the pleasure of my client. This was the easiest money I had ever earned in my life and as I crossed the car park and walked into the supermarket I worked out my hourly rate of pay for the job... around one thousand five hundred pounds. Ten jobs per week like that would be nice, half a million a year. This was another world as my mind turned somersaults.

I bought the best bottle of champagne Tesco had to offer, a Veuve Clicquot Vintage at just under forty pounds and a selection box of sushi. I figured I owed myself a little indulgence and a little alcohol to help me sleep and as I drove home I wondered how many John 0057s there were out there and how Mistress Zeta could possibly make their acquaintance.

Chapter One

My name is Jessica, or Mistress Zeta as my clients prefer to call me and I humiliate men for a living, I specialise in financial domination. Never did I think as I worked my way through school and college with decent grades that I would be doing the sort of thing I'm doing now but the reality is my hourly rate far exceeds that of a brain surgeon, a top doctor or even the prime minister of England.

I started out as a dancer in a club, it was good money and at first I quite enjoyed it and I suppose I fell into my current profession by accident as I began to watch and study the men, my clients who came to watch me.

It was another Saturday night at the club, the smell of sweat and alcohol permeated the thick air and I struggled to breathe. As I finished another spot on the pole I was tired and my feet ached and I took a sharp intake of breath as I looked at the clock by the bar and realised it was only one after midnight. I felt like crap and had at least another four hours to go before the club closed. I desperately wanted to go home to bed and sleep but of course I couldn't, so I tried to check out some of the customers looking for easy money targets. I realised quite quickly that we had a bad crowd in. There were some large groups of men, stag nights or birthday parties; some were slumped over, almost sleeping on the tables. These types of men could sometimes be easy prey as they were urged on by their mates to follow the girls into the private dance areas where they would hand over their money and sometimes fall asleep. That happened quite a lot and it never ceased to amaze me how stupid they were handing over a wad of ten and twenty pound notes to watch a girl they could hardly focus on and then pass out. But they could also be dangerous and a complete waste of time and effort, too drunk and disorientated to know where their wallets were and often abusive and insulting. I sat by the bar drinking an orange juice as I watched a group of rowdy men eyeing up each dancer and then loudly announcing their marks out of ten. One of the dancers was a little flat chested and obviously quite wary of them and she didn't dance well. They booed and hissed her and she left the stage almost in tears and of course nobody followed her to the private booths which are where you make the decent money. There was no doubt about it, we were animals in an obscene cattle market and I hated it and loathed every man in the room, I'd had seven long years doing this and I wanted a way out.

Strangely enough though, I did sometimes enjoy performing on the stage and of course with the experience I had, I knew exactly how to play the audience and could almost pick and choose the men who were going to get the private treatment, spotting the wealthy, generous clients a mile off. It was a game, a game played out on a female production line where some girls won and some girls lost.

I was being called up again, so I hovered by the stage preening myself and making eye contact with some of the clients I'd already chosen as likely candidates. I was in the jungle playing the mating game and I wanted the men who would pay for my den and put food in my belly.

They called my name and introduced me. The shouts and catcalls started as soon as I took the stage.

"Check out the tits on that?"

"Fucking hell mate she'll do for me."

There were the normal jeers from punters trying to intimidate you and the loners' silent stares that can freak you out if you let them.

My fake smile was plastered all over my face as I strode onto the stage as Michael Jackson's Dirty Diana started to play. I took a deep breath and focused out through the bright lights as I prepared to go into my routine which by now was second nature to me. I was about to start when one bloke shouted out loud.

"I'll give her a three, she's a three, fucking hopeless."

His mates were laughing and I stared hard at him and mouthed "fuck you." It had the desired effect as he squirmed and slunk back in his chair with his mouth firmly shut. I don't know why but I mouthed a few more obscenities to him and called him a loser. I started to dance and felt a real adrenalin rush course through my body as I grabbed the steel pole and threw myself upside down. I could see the loser concentrating on me as his mates tried to urge him to trade more insults with me but he slunk lower again into his seat as I released one hand from the pole and gave him the stiff finger. I confess I was enjoying the effect I was having on him as I clung to the pole with the inside of my thighs.

There were more compliments coming from his Neanderthal pals as my first song came to an end and the second one picked up the pace. I was now completely focused on the loser though couldn't understand or explain why. I climbed up the pole and lent back, flicking the clasp of my nearly there top unveiling my surgically enhanced chest and if I say so myself, the surgeon did a first class job. More compliments from his mates but a stony silence from the loser as I slid seductively down the pole now dressed in just my G-string and stilettos. I leant my back against the pole and reached above me, I looked them in the eyes one by one before I grabbed the pole just above my head and pulled my whole body upwards and backwards giving a perfect view of my flimsy lace G-string which left very little to the imagination.

They were clapping now and some were on their feet but the loser was still glued to his seat with barely a smile on his face. I had finished my show hanging upside down on the pole using only the pressure of my thighs and held the pose for some seconds and I knew I was a winner, always a winner, they were so damned predictable, mission accomplished.

I slid down the pole replaced my top and looked at the line-up of men standing waiting to join me in the private booths. To my sheer amazement there was the loser first in line. I was shocked!

I was caught like a rabbit in the headlights, I was stunned, what was this man doing standing in the line to pay me money for a private dance when all I had done was abuse him? The man didn't look wealthy, he wasn't handsome or fit looking and yet

I saw something in his eyes that told me he needed this private performance more than the others in line and so I took a deep breath and led him away by the lapel of his cheap sports jacket.

They say there are moments that change your life and while that might sound a little dramatic that evening was certainly changing something in me. It was as if I was programmed to know exactly what this man wanted, more of the same that I'd given him as he'd wriggled in his seat. So that's what I did, I verbally abused him for twenty minutes as he handed me ten pound notes as if he had a mini printing press in his pocket. I danced a little trying to tease and seduce him and he even told me to keep my top on which was all rather bizarre but it wasn't until I called him the vilest names under the sun that his wallet opened and he laid the money on the table. I remember thinking at the time that the money was counterfeit or he would snatch it all back at the end of the session and make a dash for the door before security could catch up with him. The pile of cash was growing like a mini mountain and was about to spill onto the floor. I decided it was time to draw the performance to a close and was more than a little nervous of what the conclusion would be to the strangest show I'd ever given.

But he didn't run and he didn't snatch the cash back and thanked me and politely said goodbye before dashing from the booth. I gathered up the cash and walked quickly towards the dressing rooms.

I sat down in the changing room and took stock of what had just happened. I was confused more than anything at how and why a man could get sexual gratification out of a situation like that. I had called him names, insulted and abused him and he'd loved every second. I called myself a dancer but deep down knew I was a stripper and I hated the word and the industry. I thought long and hard as I removed my make-up and stared into the mirror. Was this a way out, another way to pay the bills and afford the luxuries that a big salary provided?

As I drove home I began worrying about the money. It looked and felt fine to me and yet why would anyone pay that sort of money for what amounted to abuse? Surely it had to be dodgy?

I paid for a few things with his cash the following day and each shop accepted it without question, one store even scanning two notes under an ultraviolet light counterfeit machine which I admit made my heart skip a beat. The loser had handed me three hundred and sixty pounds that night, one of the biggest paying private dances I'd ever had and it was real, kosher currency.

Over the next few days I changed my perception of the industry and how I could make the most of what was normally a real shady business. The loser made me think and analyse exactly what it was I was doing and before long I was researching the phrase dominatrix on the internet. I needed to find out exactly what it was he'd enjoyed so much. At the end of a long Google surfing session one particular passage hit me full in the face and there it was in black and white.

> A **dominatrix** or **mistress** is a woman who takes the dominant role in bondage, discipline (in the sexual-fetish sense of the word) and sadomasochism, or BDSM. A common form of address for a submissive to a dominatrix is "mistress", "ma'am", "domina" or "maîtresse". The role of a dominatrix need not involve physical pain or even sexual contact toward the submissive; her domination can be verbal, involving humiliating tasks and servitude.

You could have knocked me over with a feather, the writer of the piece clearly stating that the dominatrix can dominate certain submissives with verbal or humiliating tasks.

Looking back I realise now that it was a crossroads in my business life and I promised myself that I would look into the subject in more detail. However, at that particular juncture in time I was preoccupied by something else too. My sexual appetite was growing. I put it down to being constantly surrounded by the thought and talk of sex, after all I was paid to arouse men most of my waking hours and so it made my working day different to the average office temp.

I had always had a high sex drive even from my early teens but since my experience with the loser and the more hours I worked I felt sexier and more confident and my sexual appetite increased.

I was going through batteries for my drawer of weapons at an unsavoury speed, 'seeing to myself' (as I liked to call it) at least twice a day and also found myself giving sexier private dances to those men I found really attractive. I will state here and now though, that I never slept with any of the customers at the club or performed sexual favours. Each private dance was always no contact. For me that was strictly taboo and I would never cross that line into prostitution even though lots of the girls did.

The talk in the changing rooms was always around relationships or sex, a lot of the girls were sleeping with the customers and even sleeping with each other and I decided I was losing out on the action. I wanted sex, I was surrounded by it but although I was propositioned almost on a daily basis my activity would not evolve around anything or anyone associated with the club. This was strictly a no-no.

There was an incredibly good-looking guy at my gym and after being introduced through friends to his personal training, we started to chat and realised we were both after the same thing.. sex although at first nobody would dare to suggest that. It was no holds barred when we found out our mutual needs were identical at the end of a particularly hard personal training session. The chemistry was electric and every time he had corrected my posture or innocently touched me during the session it was like a jolt! I could feel my body yearning for him, the thoughts I was having whilst he was helping me stretch out were enough to make even me blush!

The feeling building up inside me was incredible, I couldn't look him in the eye, he had the warmest smile and the most kissable looking lips, I honestly think the way I had been looking at him he knew I wanted him badly.

And then it happened. I was his last client for the evening and after a particular long work out I told him I was taking a shower before I headed home. He said he was just going to lock the main door as there were only the two of us left in the building. I blushed and bit my lip. Why was he doing that? He'd never locked the main door before. Looking up into his eyes I paused for a second then turned and walked towards the ladies changing room. The signals were crystal clear and as I walked away I could feel his eyes boring into me. As I reached the door I turned around and once again looked at him suggestively hoping he would understand what I wanted.

Once in the room I ripped my clothes off and grabbed my Chanel body wash, I wanted to be ready for him because after that hard work out on the gym floor I'm sure I was smelling less feminine than usual.

As the hot water cascaded over my body gradually the steam started to fill the room. As I was working over my shoulders with the lather I thought I heard the door open. I stood still breathing hard and yet praying it would be him and that he'd picked up on the exact message I had been giving out.

"Why don't you let me do that?" I heard

Oh my God, I thought, he's here and it's really going to happen.

I turned around giving him a full frontal view and smiled as I realised that he was naked too. His body was incredible despite the steam. It was so toned, so tight and muscular and my legs almost gave way as he walked forward and took hold of me grabbing the back of my neck and kissing me hard as his other hand slid around my waist and onto my back as he pulled me into him. I moaned into his mouth as he cupped my right cheek tracing a lone finger over the back of my pussy teasing me as my hands naturally encircled his waist. I knew what was coming as I eased myself up onto my tiptoes urgently pulling him closer as I dragged my nails along his flesh feeling his hard cock pressing against my stomach. His finger had found my clit and as he worked on me he kissed me even harder. I swear my knees nearly buckled but just as I thought I was going to collapse he moved his hand from my neck and grabbed my other buttock, lifting me. Instinctively I put my arms around his neck and with ease wrapped my legs around his waist. He positioned me perfectly as I felt the hard tip of his cock at the entrance of my pussy and without the need to use his hand for guidance he lowered me slowly and entered me. The sensation was absolutely mind blowing. My back was crushed against the cold tiled wall as the hot water continued to flow over our bodies as he thrust in and out kissing me all the while. I caught occasional glimpses of him through the steam and as his rhythm quickened he stopped kissing me and stared into my eyes. I could feel the familiar warm tingling feeling starting to course through my body.

"Oh my God," I gasped. "I'm going to come."

"Good girl, come for me Jess, come for me."

He purred, slowing down as he kissed me again. And then it started, what felt like the hardest and most satisfying orgasm I was ever going to have and he sensed it as my whole body started to tense up. He smiled a wicked smile as he thrust into me even harder and my back slapped off the cold tiles. I was nearly there, and I begged him to keep going.

"Stop," he said.

"What the hell?"

What was he doing? No don't stop I wanted to scream out but he was already lowering me to the floor and as he reached roughly for my wrist, spun me round to face the wall and kicked my legs apart as he nipped the back of my neck with his teeth. I realised this was how he wanted to take me and I loved every glorious second of it. I arched my back as he entered me again filling me deeper than I had ever experienced before. With one hand on my hip and the other supporting his weight on the wall he started again, this time faster and harder and I sensed he wasn't far away from climaxing himself as those sensational feelings welled up inside me yet again and he thrust into me all the more.

It was truly amazing, hard passionate sex. We were like animals and best of all we were in sync as we climaxed together and as a unit slid slowly onto the floor of the shower room as the hot water continued to flow all over us as we lay exhausted gasping for breath.

That was the first of many and I couldn't get enough of him. He was so good at everything he did to me even just kissing him would make me so uncontrollably wound up . I couldn't wait for our regular training sessions which after ten minutes of stretching and a few dozen sit ups would descend into full debauchery, it was getting more and more difficult to keep our hands off each other and soon the gym work was non-existent and we even dispensed with the stretches, it was fantastic. The more sex I had with Mark the more I wanted – actually NEEDED! Even if Mark was shattered after a full day of workouts I would still be trying it on. For the first time in my life I wanted sex more than a man could handle.

I struggled with my conscience at first and fought the urge but knew I had to find myself a second 'fuck buddy,' or as I prefer 'friend with benefits' as they are called these days. It is a very simple concept and one I have no problem with now, but at the time my head was telling me that those types of girls would no doubt garner a certain reputation. Throughout history, from Biblical times, girls who professed to enjoy and practise sex were looked down on and called harlots and whores, while men of a similar ilk were studs and gigolos and placed on a pedestal and looked up to by men and women alike. It just wasn't fair and I needed something to give me a push and tell my angelic gremlin who sat on my right shoulder to take a hike and let me get my fix.

I turned up at Mark's apartment one night yearning for some naughty fun. I thought I would give him a little surprise and dressed in a Burberry mac with only my G-string, suspender belt and stockings underneath. I wore my favourite heels and spent some time carefully applying my make-up, all the while recalling the first time I'd had the pleasure of getting to know him in the shower, it was my 'go to' memory, it was so unexpected and perfect.

As soon as he opened the door I sensed he wasn't in the mood but nevertheless I had a concealed secret weapon with which to bring him round.

He asked to take my coat and I let it fall to the floor. He looked me up and down and I waited for the fireworks to begin anticipating his sexy grin and the 'I'm going to screw you' look.

"Can we have a little dinner first," he said apologetically, unwilling to catch my eye. "I'm starving."

I couldn't believe it but tried to hide my disappointment and if I'm honest, embarrassment. I sat there at the dinner table in practically my birthday suit eating the pasta meal he had prepared. Mark explained he had recently come out of a long relationship and wanted to take things a 'little slower' as he put it. Strangely enough I knew exactly what he meant.

I really liked Mark, he really was my type of guy and we got on incredibly well, especially when we went out to town on a

Saturday night or just to a restaurant. We were connected, not lovey dovey or anything like that, we didn't act like we were together but friends who weren't aware of our arrangement could tell we had something going on between the sheets. Most people argue when alcohol is thrown into the equation but not us, we were just more sexually aroused when we were a little tipsy, waking up in the morning unable to find our clothes, my torn panties lying in the middle of the floor where he had ripped them off.

Mark had been spontaneous when it came to sex too. Sometimes I would walk into his gym or his apartment and he would literally rip my clothes off, slam me against the wall and take me like he'd never seen a girl before and I positively loved it. But lately I had begun to realise those moments were few and far between and didn't happen regularly enough for me. I was also developing other feelings for Mark too, feelings of a sensitive nature and at that stage in my life I didn't want to fall in love and definitely didn't want to settle down or get involved. I understood exactly where he was coming from and the Burberry incident as I called it was the catalyst to finding a new 'buddy'.

My new 'no strings attached' boyfriend number two took a lot of prep work, and by that I mean the type of lengths a guy would go to in order to bed a woman. I kid you not, I had found my target but he was hard work. We went out on quite a few dates and ever the gentleman he would always kiss me goodbye at the end of the night and push me into a taxi on my own when all I wanted to do was find out what colour sheets were on his bed. Please don't judge, ladies, we have all been there!

I shared the gossip with my two close girlfriends and told them how much I wanted to seal the deal with my latest target. He was a professional sportsman (I won't go any further than that) with a body to die for; drop dead gorgeous with a personality to match and the girls adored him. My girlfriends couldn't believe how sexed up and frustrated I was and when they told me I was more like a man when it came to dealing with these feelings I suppose they were right, it was true; I was casual in my approach and attitude and apparently quite aloof after sex, maybe even cold. We shared secrets, talked a lot and at times they made me feel a little guilty about what I was doing – unintentionally of course. We talked about the intimate side of a relationship and I admitted I wasn't much of a cuddler and it was purely the physical side that really did it for me. I certainly didn't mean to come across as an ice queen (the unfortunate name I had been called more than once) but when I wanted a man I was prepared to do what it took to get him into bed, except of course if they were married, that was a no go for me.

I persevered with the sportsman figuring the wait would be well worth it and listened to his longwinded details of his training sessions and where he was playing that weekend, he was older than his years, quite sensible and a bit of a father figure I suppose and at times he was hard work. It was all part of the tiring ground work that I was hoping would pay off. He was a handsome specimen, very tall and very muscular, same height as Mark but slightly older and a hell of a unit. I stood looking up at him in a pub one night feeling really turned on. I stand at just five feet tall so the thought of a big strong man taking me and doing what he wanted with me was such an attractive thought.

After plenty of meets for coffee, long walks in the park with his dog, nights in the pub and a couple of decent restaurants he finally asked me over to his place one Friday night.

"Just the two of us," he said. I sensed this was it and I really was excited.

It started well as he announced he had a hot tub in the garden and carried out a bottle of champagne, some glasses and two fluffy white robes. He pointed me in the direction of the bathroom and told me to change. Wow I thought; this man knows the real meaning of seduction, such class.

He was already in the tub when I walked outside. The steam was rising into the cool night air and a thick layer of bubbles covered his modesty. He'd strategically placed cinnamon candles all around the garden and it looked and smelled like something from paradise, a real Garden of Eden.

We were in the tub for about twenty minutes, no more and the champagne buzz was starting to work its magic on me.

"Take me upstairs," I whispered to him but he shook his head.

"In a little while," he said,

We stood up in unison as he wrapped the thick robe around me and gave me a long lingering kiss. We retreated into the large sitting room and he put on some music until we finished the bottle of champagne.

It was time and he leaned over and kissed me so passionately that I guessed we might not even make it up the stairs.

I stood in front of him looking into his eyes I opened his robe slightly and pushed it over his huge broad shoulders leaving it still tied around his thick waist. A sexy beat had hit the track list so I stepped away, untied my hair and let the robe fall to the floor. He knew I was a dancer and often said he would like to see my work so I thought, okay, here goes. He stood there mesmerised as I walked up close to him keeping eye contact. I pushed him back against the sofa and parted his legs so as I could dance close.

"No touching," I whispered with a naughty wink.

He said nothing just slowly shook his head, I started to dance. Within just a few minutes he untied his robe slipping it off around him and groaned as he started to stroke his rising cock.

My ground work was finally going to get me laid I thought as he flopped over onto his back which was my signal to straddle him. As I moved onto the sofa ready to position myself where I had waited so long to be I ran my nails up the inside of his leg which aroused him even more and he pulled me down towards his stiff cock. It was tantalisingly close as it brushed against my clitoris but as he leaned close towards me kissing my neck he whispered in my ear.

"Not yet Jessica."

'Oh God what now' I screamed to myself

It was positively torture and I recall thinking that this night, despite the wait was going to be one of the best nights of my life. He'd purposely teased and seduced me these last few months, he was an expert in the art and he had me exactly where he wanted me as I squirmed wanting him inside me.

He then announced he wanted to go upstairs. NO! Was he joking? I remained optimistic as he lifted me up, took my hand and led me naked up the stairs. He walked me into his impressive bedroom and pushed me onto the huge bed and as I lay there looking up into his face as he seemed to study my naked form a wicked grin pulled across his face. This was it, he was going to join me on the bed and slip his rock hard cock inside me and I would almost explode there and then. I closed my eyes in anticipation, every nerve ending tingling with expectancy as I felt his weight lower onto the mattress. And what did he do? He stuck his head between my bloody legs! Now... I am well aware how pleasurable an expert tongue is when it locates a throbbing clitoris and I know how some girls can prefer this to the actual sex act but for me, quite frankly I can take it or leave it and when I do find the urge for my man to go down on me he has to be my man and not a 'friend' or someone I've loosely dated for a couple of months. This is the most intimate part of my body and without sounding prudish that act needs to be performed by a very special person and only when the time is right. The timing was definitely not right and this man was not special. I could feel myself becoming anxious and clamming up, quickly losing motivation. I tried to urge him on top of me but he wouldn't have it and continued to lick like his life depended on it. It started to sound disgusting; I was beginning to feel repulsed. Furthermore, I don't think he'd ever studied a diagram of the female reproductive organs or ever been told where the clitoris was located because he was a million miles away from it and instead seemed hell bent on how far he could get his tongue up inside me. I was losing the will to live as I gasped out loudly that I wanted him inside me but still he resisted and licked and sucked for all he was worth. There was only one course of action, panting I yelled out.

"That was amazing! Oh my!"

Yes that's right, I'm not proud to say it but I faked an orgasm and it seemed to do the trick as he lifted himself up and grinned the grin that said 'I'm the man' when it comes to cunninglingus. Jesus Christ I was so annoyed and my passion and desire that had built up to a crescendo during the evening was wilting like an autumn rose. This large strong powerful man should have been throwing me around the bedroom and fucking me in every position he could think of. But no, his fifteen minute tongue session had obviously worked him up to the point of no return because I immediately found myself bent over in the doggy position as he thrust into me and quickly brought himself to an orgasm.

He lay panting on the bed, out of breath and I could hardly look at him. Talk about an anti-climax???

"Was it good for you?" he said.

"Yes," I lied. "Breathtaking."

I wanted to say it was terrible and totally not worth the work I had put in, not to mention the time I had had to wait. What a disappointment, but being nice and considerate I didn't want to hurt his feelings. Maybe we could talk this through and I'd put him straight on a few things?

I saw him a few times more, convinced that the sex would get better but it didn't. It was more of the same, full on tongue play and a quick, romp each time. I tried telling him that it wasn't my thing but he wouldn't listen. On reflection the sex was bad, the word awkward fits perfectly and even though I thought it was going to be amazing, it never was.

After each physical encounter I felt more and more uncomfortable and put off by the whole thing and made several excuses to avoid other dates with him and as he continued to text and call me without reply he eventually got the message.

This was hard for me as I felt frustrated and confused, not sure of what it was I wanted out of the relationship. I had Mark, he was like a best friend to me and although the sex was electrifying and I wanted more, I knew he didn't. I was developing sensitive feelings which naturally occur during prolonged sexual activity and I tried to fight them and keep them under control. That's why I had taken another lover but that turned out to be a major disappointment.

I was so frustrated and I could feel Mark pulling away, I didn't know what I wanted anymore and I began to see less and less of him and I think he eventually met someone else, a nice girl with not such a high sex drive I suppose. I consoled myself with my drawer full of toys and made sure I had a healthy supply of batteries.

The time was perfect for David to step into my life.

Chapter Two

I met David through a day time sales job I had and when I left the company he continued to email me. He seemed a nice, normal guy and I suppose I was quite attracted to him but I was more than aware he was thirteen years older than me and at first didn't want to get involved. He kept asking me out and although at first I politely declined I talked it over one night with one of my friends and decided to give it a go. He was quite kind towards me and also a little old fashioned which I really liked and as we dated more and more he began to grow on me.

David knew I had been paid off from the sales job and knew I had a house with a mortgage and several times asked what I was doing for a living. For some reason I couldn't bring myself to tell him about the club and my dancing, I was probably petrified that he'd overreact. So I lied, I told him I had a well-paid bar job and that I was soon to be promoted. For a time he seemed to buy it and stopped asking, thank God he never asked what or where the bar was. I'm not ashamed of what it was I did for a living but I'm more than aware that some people would see me as less of a person or cheap if I told them I danced with next to nothing on for the pleasure of men. Some people even look on pole dancing as akin to prostitution which is understandable because I know that there are some girls that do entertain their clients in that way if the price is right. However, a large majority of girls in the pole or lap dancing clubs restrict their activity solely to dancing which means no physical contact of any type. In general my dancing colleagues were well educated, hardworking, independent girls and although we are well paid for what we did I don't think we should be judged on the actions of a minority. There are many of the girls who are the breadwinners in their family and this is the sole reason they work, in order that they can give their family the luxuries, and holidays that perhaps their husbands or partners can't.

We had been dating for six months when David asked me to move in with him. It seemed like a good idea at the time and I thought about renting my house out, which would still give me the financial independence I needed. Ever the gentleman David sealed the deal by saying that he had booked us a holiday in Tenerife and he had instructed an estate agent to find a tenant while we were lying in the sun enjoying ourselves. It sounded perfect so I agreed and left everything in the capable hands of the agent while we headed off to the airport. This was the beginning of a new chapter of my life and I was looking forward to it, even though I had only stayed with David a few nights a week I didn't give it a second thought.

By this time I had strong feelings for him and was fully prepared for a long term commitment. The flight was perfect, David had booked good seats in advance with plenty of legroom and we shared a bottle of champagne somewhere over the Bay of Biscay. As we arrived at our destination I couldn't have been happier. He had booked a stunning five star hotel, just yards from the beach on a tranquil part of the island. We unpacked and headed down to the pool to relax, he said we could grab the last few hours of sun and take a few cocktails at the all-inclusive pool bar.

I had dressed for the pool in a bikini and slipped a kaftan around me while I walked through the hotel reception area. We sat at the pool bar on the seats that were half emerged in the pool. It was a perfect end to a perfect day as I nursed a cool Pina-Colada and David enjoyed a gin and tonic. I was watching the sun rapidly disappear behind the tall building of the hotel and suggested we catch the last of the rays. He agreed and we finished our drinks and made our way over to the sun loungers. I started to lay out my towel and book then removed my kaftan.

"What is the fucking hell is that?" I heard David say angrily.

I looked around to see what had upset him.

"What honey?" I said

He was looking directly at me.

"What the hell is that you are wearing?" he said. "You look like a cheap whore."

I looked at him in disbelief, shocked because he'd never said anything like that before. At first I thought he was playing some sort of cheap joke but when I looked into his hard cold eyes I could see no humour. I could feel the colour draining from my face as I stalled and stuttered.

"I don't know what you mean," I said, "it's a bikini David and we're by a pool, that's what girls wear at the poolside."

He stared at me, his eyes were tiny and vicious looking and I'd never seen him like that before.

"Put it back on now," he snarled through his teeth.

I looked down at the kaftan on the lounger and pointed at it.

"What? Put what back on, my kaftan, are you serious?"

I pointed across the pool.

"There's a woman topless over there for Christ's sake."

I was furious as I looked at all the near naked bodies on display. He had no right to say this to me, to order me to cover up. I wanted to take a stand and front him out but became aware that I was also trembling slightly... I was scared. For the first time in my life I was scared of a man and I was ashamed to say it. I tried to fight the feeling and concentrated on being angry. I told myself I was wearing a damn bikini and not a G-string, nor was I topless. It was just a nice, designer gold bikini. What gave him the right to say what I had to wear? But it wasn't working; my legs were like jelly now and I started to feel sick as I saw his face getting redder by the minute. He came towards me and grabbed my wrist hard. He took me by surprise.

"Put the fucking thing back on now," he hissed.

He leaned across the sun lounger picked up my kaftan and threw it at me. I could feel the tears welling up and the dreaded lump in my throat made it hard for me to swallow. I buckled, pushed back the tears and pulled the kaftan over my shoulders.

He started throwing our things into his bag as he smiled sweetly. "Now darling, we are going to the shops to buy you another swimsuit."

It was as if nothing was wrong, as if it was the most natural thing in the world to humiliate your girlfriend on the first day of your first ever holiday. I was totally gobsmacked, struck dumb in disbelief. It was Dr Jekyll and Mr Hyde; I had never seen this side of him before.

But nevertheless I followed him like a little lost sheep as he led me out of the hotel to a small boutique not far from the entrance and I still didn't say a word. We walked into the shop as I stood in stunned silence.

"I need a swim suit for my girlfriend," he said to the assistant.

She looked me up and down as I stared at the floor fighting the tears that welled up behind my eyelids. I was mortified and more so because I hadn't done anything wrong – I was sure of that. He pulled my kaftan to the side and exposed my bikini as if to say to the assistant, 'do you see what I mean'? He made me feel so cheap, worse than any customer at the club could make me feel and believe me some of them can make you feel pretty awful. What was I doing here? I just wanted to go home. I was confused and upset and it was only the first day. I started to panic. I was 3000 miles from home, no family or friends to run to, and no one I'd even spoken to by the pool for a shoulder to cry on.

I tried on a couple of swimsuits of David's choice and left the boutique with a sober coloured tankini with matching frumpy bottoms. It was simply horrible and I was angry at myself for letting him make me feel that way. And here's the strange bit. As I walked towards the lift in the foyer and the doors closed I also began to question what I had been wearing at the time, wondering if perhaps my gold bikini had exposed a little more flesh than was decent.

Once back at the room David started to unpack my clothes from the case examining them all, particularly my bikinis and short crop t-shirts. He threw two or three items onto the floor.

"Can't you see why I was mad at you Jessica?" he said.

I didn't speak; I couldn't even look at him.

"I didn't want others to look at you and think the same as I did when you took off that kaftan. You have a beautiful body but it's for me and me only."

His smile was sickly sweet, as he leered at me.

"You understand don't you?"

I couldn't look at him as I mumbled some sort of acknowledgement that I agreed with him. That night he wined and dined me as if I was a princess. He was attentive and generous and loving, the man I had fallen in love with once again and I honestly couldn't understand where the horrible, mean bully had come from. As the alcohol began to kick in I even wondered if I had imagined it all.

But I hadn't imagined any of it. It was just the beginning. It happened again towards the end of the holiday when he caught a man looking at me while we were having dinner. This was apparently my fault! His eyes went small again as he spat insults at me. I defended myself saying I couldn't help it if someone looked at me. Wasn't he pleased if other men found me attractive? Big mistake.

"He's looking at you because you're looking at him," he roared, "aren't you?"

"Of course I'm not David, don't be silly," I said. "I didn't even notice him until you pointed him out."

Other diners were beginning to take notice now as David had raised his voice.

"You're a lying bitch Jess, a lying fucking bitch," he said.

I could feel the tears welling up again, I felt like throwing up and my appetite had disappeared instantly. Why was he doing this? I thought to myself, I haven't done anything wrong. I pushed the salad around my plate while he continued to abuse and ridicule me for the next twenty minutes until I could stand it no more and ran from the restaurant in tears.

Then the next day he was normal again, sweet, kind, loving David, claiming it was my dress that had brought the unwanted attention. I had been wearing a bloody maxi dress.

The Jekyll and Hyde characters resurfaced several times on that holiday and although I tried my best to make sense of what was happening, I couldn't. At first I did look at what I was doing or rather what I had been wearing but I was the same person wearing exactly the same style of clothes when David had first met me, when by his own admission he'd been attracted towards me. Just what was it he was saying, I couldn't look nice when I was in public? This unnerved me. I'd heard about domineering men like this, even watched them on the big screen in cinemas. The same movie came to me over and over again. Was I now 'Sleeping With The Enemy'? Was I the character Julia Roberts portrayed in that powerful movie? Was David turning into the character Patrick Bergin played? Did David have some sort of obsessive compulsive disorder? These were the questions I asked myself over and over again during the four hour flight home while David whispered sweet nothings in my ear as he plied me with the most expensive champagne on board the aeroplane.

When we returned home the estate agents had let my house, they had taken a deposit, signed the lease and the family were moving in the following Monday. I should have been happy but a wave of dread passed over me as I thanked the estate agents and agreed to move my personal belongings into storage by the end of the week.

I moved in with David and it was quiet for the first month and then the Tenerife nightmare started all over again. The outbursts were more frequent and he was more volatile. Everything was my fault and I was treading on eggshells and I knew it was beginning to affect my personality and my self-confidence. He was rendering me weaker by the day... he was draining my strength.

One day I came in from work and he passed a comment about how short my skirt was. It was a few inches above the knee, hardly a mini skirt.

He hadn't shouted, hadn't even raised his voice and I mistakenly thought it was just a general discussion. He was reading the newspaper, he had hardly looked at me.

"You have to be joking David," I said, "I think you need to buy yourself a pair of glasses."

He let out a deep sigh as he folded the paper and laid it on the coffee table. Then he stood and started to walk towards me. His face was emotionless and yet menacing, if that makes sense. He was only inches away from me.

"I can see perfectly well," he whispered. "I can see that you look like a fucking cheap tart and a street walker and I won't have it do you hear?"

My legs had turned to jelly and I was convinced he was about to hit me. I stood in front of him unable to form a single word. My head had stopped working and although I wanted to say so many things nothing came out. He grabbed me gently with his forefinger and thumb just above my chin and he leaned in closer.

"So the next time you go out, you wear something that is more fitting to a professional lady than a fucking whore do you hear?"

I found myself nodding in agreement before bursting into tears and running upstairs.

I knew it would get worse because it was only a matter of time before he found out what it really was I did for a living. He was asking me more and more questions about the bar I was working in and I knew I had to come clean. I picked my moment carefully, there had been no rows for quite a few days and while we enjoyed a pleasant Sunday lunch in a crowded pub somewhere in the English countryside, I plucked up the courage and told him that the bar job had come to an end, (a little white lie) and that I had started dancing in a club. What I didn't tell him was that I stripped off most of my clothes and then gyrated for customers in a private booth. David was dumbstruck; absolutely gobsmacked but thankfully he quelled his anger in the pub. He seethed and gave me the silent treatment in the car the entire way home and when we got into the house he blew up. I tried to pacify him saying it was only dancing and explained how good the money was for just a few hours work which meant I could spend more time at home with him. It didn't work. I was standing in the kitchen defending my occupation and the girls I worked with when he reached for a china mug and hurled it across the room at me. I saw it at the last minute and ducked as it struck a glancing blow on my shoulder and smashed into the wall behind me. He said I would have to quit and I surprised myself as I refused. I tried to convince him that we needed the money and said I would look for something else but there was no way I was just walking out and joining the legions of unemployed.

The following day David was back to being Mr Nice Guy and amazed me when he announced he wanted us to have a baby. Once again he was toying with my emotions but deep down the thought appealed to me. I was twenty four years of age and for the first time I was beginning to feel quite maternal and I was also thinking that if this man wanted to start a family with me then he couldn't be all that bad and he could change too, couldn't he? Even though I had these strong feelings and emotions towards having a baby there was again that feeling of dread that seemed to hang over me. Realistically should I even be entertaining the idea of bringing a child into this up and down relationship?

The baby thing wasn't mentioned much after that initial announcement. It was all strangely peaceful and yet I noticed that David started to drink more than I could ever recall. He was going out a lot with friends and coming home late. He was still demanding that I quit my job and I lied as I told him I was constantly looking for other positions. David said that the girls who worked in that sort of industry were prostitutes, the lowest of the low, vermin and cock teasers and I did not belong with them.

By now we had a dog, a little Jack Russell called Russell. He was so affectionate and really cute and within just a few weeks had very much attached himself to me as the person he showed his affection to. I wasn't surprised. I walked him and fed him and let him cuddle up to me whenever he climbed up on the settee while David hardly gave him a passing glance. But it wasn't long before I regretted bringing the little guy into the house. It wasn't the nicest environment because he was absolutely petrified when David kicked off and he started to urinate everywhere whenever David raised his voice. It absolutely broke my heart; I loved my little dog and took to walking him for hours just to get some peace.

We had a blazing row one day when David went out on a Friday night and didn't return home until lunchtime on the following day. When I asked him where he had been he told me it was none of my business and that he would stay out for as long as he wanted. I said I had no objections to him staying out as long as he told me first. I was worried about him I said, told him that I had feared the worst and he couldn't stay out all night on a whim and expect me to accept it. I could smell the sour alcohol on his breath; he was clearly still intoxicated and had been out on a huge bender. I was furious and asked where he had been.

At first he was quite defensive but then let it slip that he had been to a strip club. I couldn't believe it, only two days before he'd had a real go at the girls I worked with. Sluts, slags, harlots and whores, he'd let them have it with both barrels and now here he was admitting he was spending his hard earned money taking enjoyment from the same girls he had claimed were lower than a snake's belly.

It was my turn to shout and shout I did. I couldn't believe he could be so hypocritical but as always David turned it around and blamed something I had done to drive him to that sort of establishment and of course he shouted louder and longer and grew more and more angry and then the cups and plates started to fly. The first one missed and the second one grazed my ear. I looked up in horror as David walked towards me. He looked positively evil and I wasn't going to hang around to see what was going to happen next. I scooped up poor Russell and ran towards the bathroom slamming the door behind me and bolting it. David was hammering on the outside of the door screaming at me to let him in and I became aware of a warm wet feeling flowing over my chest as poor Russell lost control of his bladder. I started crying at that point and begged David to go away. For a few seconds I heard nothing and then David announced that if I didn't open the door he was going to kick it in. He wouldn't, I thought to myself, this was his own house and he was so fiercely proud of it, surely he wouldn't destroy something in it deliberately?

I was wrong. David started kicking at the door as I begged him to stop. The kicks were coming every few seconds getting harder and harder and I noticed the wooden frame start to buckle where it connected with the hinges. It took David no more than three minutes to smash the door in as Russell and I cowered in the shower cubical wallowing in human tears and the dog piss. Those three minutes felt like three hours and I was convinced he was about to do me some serious damage.

But he didn't. It was almost as if an inner calm had washed over him as he sat quietly on the closed toilet seat and told me that the incident was my fault and I really should stop causing these rows. He had smashed the door in to show me I couldn't run and I couldn't hide, he said. He continued to protest that he'd had a night out with his friends, nothing more.

At the end of a one-sided ten minute discussion I was agreeing with him and snivelling my apologies.

Through the tears I asked him to forgive me and he nodded as he stood and walked away.

Chapter Three

Work became my only form of release and I dreaded coming home, the only reason I returned was for Russell. When I got to work I was Zeta and I acted the part well. I was tough, forceful, confident and strong. I smiled and laughed my way through every performance trying to make it last because when it ended and those club doors closed I knew I'd be going back to the hell that my life was becoming.

I'd read the books and the magazine articles about the girls and wives locked into abusive relationships and cursed them, calling them stupid and weak for not leaving their tormentors and yet here I was in exactly the same situation and I felt as helpless as a week old kitten.

The girls at work had also shown concern as I was now becoming jumpy and unsociable, almost withdrawn. Around the customers I could fake it, but on a break or in the changing rooms I couldn't always hide the different person I now was. I couldn't bring myself to tell them the truth about David. It's difficult to explain but part of me still loved him and I was aware of wanting to protect him. The good times were still there, of course they were and even though they were few and far between I wondered if it was just a phase David was going through. He'd change I'd tell myself over and over again, he'd go back to the man I'd first fallen in love with. I was embarrassed and felt totally out of my depth with everything that was happening.

I've already said that work was a kind of escape for me but by now even that was beginning to become difficult. Every time I walked into the lounge ready to go to work he'd launch into me about what I looked like. I had changed my hair colour from platinum blonde to nearly black at his request – apparently my blonde hair was bringing me too much attention and I should have known that. David had also thrown out at least two bin liners of my clothes as he said wearing them was asking for trouble. He had battered me down and I felt lost, I didn't even argue with him anymore. It was crazy, the girls at work called me 'the posh one' as I was always immaculately groomed, well-spoken and never ever dressed like a stripper which some girls did. I wore jeans and a blazer or maxi skirts until I went into the dressing room to change, unlike some of the girls who flaunted and teased the men from the minute they walked through the doors to the club. Their behaviour carried on beyond the four walls of the club.

I walked into the club one night and the manager looked at me in surprise.

"What are you doing here?" he said. "David phoned and said you were reducing your hours, I wasn't expecting you tonight."

I was furious as my jaw almost hit the ground. I turned around and walked straight out. What the fuck was going on? It made my skin crawl that he had actually contacted the club. What was wrong with him? As I made the thirty minute drive back home my mind was in overdrive wondering what his motives were. What was he up to? When I confronted David back home he confirmed he had made the call to the club. He sat in his chair and calmly announced that he would be deciding where I worked and what hours I worked from now on. He would choose the clothes I wore and the colour of my hair if he so desired.

I could feel myself starting to shake. I felt sick and I wanted out of this piece of shit relationship. I hated my life and I hated myself. I hated me for doing this to myself and I felt trapped. I stood in front of this sick twisted man and hated him with every single part of me. I could see that he was somehow loving what he was turning me into which made the whole situation even more fucked up. As I ranted at him he stayed quiet and then picked up his newspaper and ignored me as he smirked. It was a look of triumph, he was breaking me in two and we both knew it. Once again I eventually burst into tears as I picked up Russell and went upstairs where I cried until I was physically sick.

We didn't have a meaningful conversation for three days but by then I had calmed down. Later that evening as we were watching a movie on DVD I realised I hadn't had my period. Surely not, I thought to myself. Suddenly the movie had lost its appeal as I told David I needed a little shopping.

I hopped in the car with little Russell and popped round to the supermarket. Half an hour later the thin blue line confirmed I was pregnant.

This was my worst nightmare, I thought, as I started to shake and I slumped onto the bathroom floor crying.

I cried for at least an hour before I pulled myself together and yet David hadn't even given a second thought to why I'd disappeared for so long. I walked down the stairs, I must have looked like shit but I came right out with it as soon as he looked at me.

He took the news that I was pregnant calmly although he didn't show much emotion. He said that the timing was wrong but it was clearly meant to be. I waited for a flicker of a smile, a hug or a kiss, but neither came. Instead he stood up and walked towards the kitchen as he announced he would make us both a nice cup of tea.

Things were reasonably civilised for the best part of a week though our unborn child was never mentioned more than once or twice. I began planning ahead, thinking about the gender of the child and nurseries and when I should take myself off to the doctor.

But the nightmare notched up again when towards the end of the week he phoned me and announced I had to have an abortion. I was confused and so angry. It's just as well he told me that on the phone because I swear I would have attacked him. It had been his suggestion that we started a family but he told me the time wasn't right and that there'd be better times ahead, a better time to bring a child into the world.

I put down the phone and sunk onto the floor as little Russell padded over and sat beside me. The hatred for this man was growing by the second. My whole body ached as anger coursed through my veins.

For the next two weeks David played the part of Mr Practical. Was there no end to the characters this man could play? From dawn till dusk he badgered me gently about the practicalities of an abortion and how it would be better for everyone in the long run. I so wanted this child but eventually he wore me down and I agreed to go through with the termination. He said he would be there with me to support me every step of the way and true to his word he accompanied me when I went to the hospital and they examined me for the first time.

The doctor in charge of procedure was vile, he made me feel terrible, constantly questioning me, asking me if I really understood what I was doing? I could feel David's eyes burning into me as I looked at the floor.

"Yes I understand, I want it done as soon as possible."

I couldn't look at the doctor and I felt disgusted with myself. I had been raised a Catholic and I muttered.

"Believe me this is ripping my heart out."

Eventually the doctor gave up on his lecture as he walked out of the consultation room and said someone would sort out the dates. I burst into tears as the door closed and David remained in his seat.

They scheduled me in the following Friday and I asked David if he could come with me. He said he would drive me there but would have to leave soon after as he was playing golf. It was a regular Friday ritual for David and even an abortion wasn't going to change his plans.

He drove me there and I told him to drop me at the entrance to the hospital.

As he drove away he wound down the window and wished me luck. I couldn't believe it. I absolutely hated him!

I was shown into a room where several girls sat crying. No one said a word, their pain was obvious but there were no sympathetic nurses or orderlies, no counsellors... nothing.

It was the longest day of my life. They gave me drugs which would cause the womb to contract and then I returned to the room where more tears flowed and the girls sat like zombies. I was the last one in the room as one by one the girls were examined and sent home. I asked the nurses why I couldn't go and was simply told I wasn't finished. I had been there over twelve hours and I was shaking and sweating but refused painkillers even though I was in severe discomfort. I was eventually allowed to leave and I telephoned David who picked me up soon after.

By Sunday afternoon I couldn't move off the bed and the pain was indescribable. I had been more or less on my own since David had picked me up from the hospital on Friday evening. He'd golfed again on Saturday and went out for a few pints on the Saturday night. On Sunday morning he left early saying he could squeeze eighteen holes in before lunchtime. I was really quite worried by this point and hated David with a passion. I took whatever painkillers I could find and hoped the waves of pain would subside. I drifted in and out of sleep and by now was bleeding heavily.

Finally I heard the front door open and called on David to come quickly. He strolled into the bedroom as if there was nothing wrong and asked what was up.

I was in floods of tears and told him the pain was like nothing I had ever experienced in my life.

"God you overreact," he said, "are you trying to make me feel bad?"

He was shouting.

I couldn't believe it, this was my fault? Is that what he was saying? I screamed at him to get out and reached for my mobile phone ringing the number I had been given at the hospital. I told the nurse about the abdominal pains and the bleeding and she asked if anyone could drive me to the hospital or did I need an ambulance. I told her I would manage.

After I cleaned myself up and changed I fought against the pain and managed to make it down the stairs. David was in the kitchen making himself something to eat. I walked past the kitchen door quietly, opened the front door and made it outside. I managed to ease myself into the car and drove away. David had a clear view of the car from the kitchen window and I half expected him to come running after me. At least he would surely call me? My mobile phone was on the passenger seat next to me in the twenty minutes it took me to reach the hospital. The call never came.

Three hours later I was seen and told the bad news that there had been a complication. The consultant explained that it all should have 'happened' before I was discharged on the Friday evening. The womb lining should have broken down and been lost along with the embryo. The consultant explained that pain and heavy bleeding was normal but the duration of the termination was not. They gave me the drug again and made me wait: I was then discharged.

It happened all over again. More pain, severe bleeding and three more days in bed until I could stand the pain no more. David took me to the hospital that particular time; he had no choice as I crawled through the lounge on all fours and begged him to take me. He seemed concerned at one point as he led me through the hospital corridors to the consulting room before he vanished without trace. I was there most of the day and given yet more drugs.

I took a taxi home later that day as David's mobile was out of reception range. He arrived home later that evening dressed in his golfing gear.

Eventually, after another visit to the hospital they were forced to take me to theatre to complete the procedure with surgery.

It had been nearly six weeks since the first procedure, six weeks of hell on earth wondering if when I crawled into bed at night I would make it through to the next morning.

By this point the writing was on the wall. I wasn't even allowed to talk to David about it, because it upset him. How the hell could he be like this? I couldn't believe I had fallen in love with such a selfish, self-centred, domineering man who put a game of golf over my health and emotions.

When my dear Mum visited me after the operation I told her that I had miscarried. I couldn't bear to tell her that the truth.

I wanted to leave but as most women who have been in this situation know, it can be difficult. For several weeks I convinced myself to simply walk out on him but I couldn't. It was the line of least resistance to stay put, the easiest thing to do. He continued to abuse me mentally and choose my clothes and throw things at me but then he was always nice to me a day or two afterwards and things went back to normal. But recent events and his no-show in the hospital on so many occasions began to gnaw away at me and I resented him more and more. I needed to be strong and pick my moment, perhaps call on some assistance from a friend or two.

As if by luck or perhaps divine intervention one of my friends called me on a wet Wednesday night and announced that the old crowd were meeting up for her twenty fifth birthday. I politely refused at first because I knew David would object, but she wouldn't take no for an answer. I told her I would be there and pressed 'end call'.

David did object but eventually he gave in and said I could go out for a few hours and he would collect me from the bar at eleven pm, a suitable time by his standards. Once again he chose my clothes and even told me to tie up my hair but he allowed me out and even drove me to the bar dropping me right outside the door. It was all very surreal as he kissed me gently on the lips and said goodbye. Everything seemed so normal, little did we both know the bombshell I was about to drop a few hours from now.

It was great to be in the old scene again, the party was in full swing and as the drinks flowed I remembered what it was like to laugh hard again. This man had stifled me for almost a year and as we joked and danced in the bar it was as if I had somehow managed to turn back the clock. It was fast approaching the witching hour and the girls moaned and begged me to stay on longer than eleven o'clock plying me with drinks to bring the old Jessica back, the Jessica who loved to party and have fun with her friends

David phoned spot on ten thirty to say he was leaving and I should be at the door in exactly thirty minutes. I was more than tipsy at this point and slurring my words. He started shouting at me so loudly that I became aware that my friends could actually hear him. At one point I even held my mobile at arm's length so that the world could hear the abuse he was hurling at me but surrounded by my friends I felt stronger.

He was ranting away on loudspeaker calling me a drunken whore and everyone within twenty yards could hear him and at that point I no longer cared. I didn't want to conceal my pain any longer, I no longer felt a need to protect or cover up for him.

I placed the handset to my mouth.

"David," I said, "fuck off; you're not going to speak to me like that anymore."

His voice climbed several decibels as he told me what was waiting for me back home.

"Didn't you hear me?" I said. "Fuck off. Fuck off for good, not just tonight but forever. It's over, I'm leaving you so don't bother picking me up because you'll be wasting your time."

I ended the call and switched off my phone. I looked around at all of my wonderful friends who by that point had been struck dumb. I grinned like a Cheshire cat then seconds later I broke down and wept like a baby. My whole body was tired, I felt fragile and scared and although I was glad I had just said what I did, I also knew I wouldn't be able to return home on my own. I had used my friends to give me the courage to end it, I had drawn on their strength and didn't care if that made me a coward because it was the only way I was going to be able to leave him.

We left the bar almost immediately and went somewhere else. That night I told my friends everything that had been happening. They vowed to help me and I made a pledge to leave David the very next day. I drank with my friends as they chatted up random groups of men and I sat strangely at ease whilst trying to come to terms with what had just happened. We moved on to a nightclub and had a ball! In the early hours of the morning we all drifted back to one of my friends' houses with takeaway pizzas then crashed in spare bedrooms and on her sofas.

Despite the hangover from hell the next day, I felt like a million dollars, as if the world's troubles had been lifted from my shoulders.

The following day I returned to the house with my best friend. Sunday was David's main day for golf and even after the dramas of the previous evening I knew he would still be out on the course.

Russell greeted me like my best friend and peed all over the front step in excitement and suddenly I was aware that I was about to kidnap a dog too.

With the help of my friend I managed to pack most of my things, Russell's bed and some of his toys. We loaded the car up and with a deep breath and a gentle push from my friend I left his house, our home, forever. I left the heartbreak and mental abuse behind there and then and as we drove out onto the roadway I wondered why I hadn't found the strength to leave him even sooner.

Chapter Four

My finances were shot to pieces. I realised that David had controlled the purse strings in our relationship too and although he had never been over mean, everything I had earned over the last year had gone into 'the house' – his house and I was left with nothing apart from the dog.

Towards the end of our relationship he had cut my hours at the club and if I needed anything I had to dip into my savings which were now also dangerously low. And yet I drew on an inner strength, a confidence that had deserted me for twelve months and was now drifting back. I'd always worked, always been proud of my independence and almost every job I'd ever applied for I'd been offered the position.

My attitude in the early weeks after I left David was 'fuck him', he wasn't going to break me, or get me down. Some days were harder than others but I felt at peace and had little Russell to keep me company. David contacted me just the once asking me to go back. Even then I detected no sincerity or desire in his voice; it was what I would describe as a half-arsed attempt to get me back. As I hung up I knew I had made the correct decision. I had never been so sure of anything in my life.

I looked at the screen of the mobile phone and searched through my contacts locating the hairdresser. I booked myself in the following day to get rid of my black hair, a depressing reminder of the relationship I had just left behind.

Three bleach baths later and a full head of highlights and a different person looked back at me in the mirror. Jessica was back and enjoying life and the next thing I did was ask the manager of the club to reinstate my lost shifts which he seemed happy enough to do even though there was a crisis sweeping the country and jobs were being cut left right and centre. He did say that the customers were thinner on the ground and said I had to be realistic about my ability to earn. I would have to work smarter and put in longer hours to make the sort of money I had been used to pre David, which some weeks were as high as two thousand pounds.

By now, because of government influenced interest rates my mortgage payments had nearly doubled but I still felt confident and relaxed knowing that I could make good money and sleep in during the days thus putting more energy into working the customers at night. The manager had used the phrase 'work smarter' and it triggered something inside me as I remembered the guy with that weird thing for humiliation.

I knew there was more money out there for a girl who could discover a niche, a certain type of client who was cash rich or perhaps just desperate to find a girl who could fulfil his needs, satisfy his particular type of fantasy or fetish.

It was winter now and the weekday shifts were a little hit and miss due to the dark cold nights. I was sat by the bar sipping my orange juice when I heard someone walk up behind me,

"Um, excuse me," he stammered.

As I swivelled around on the stool to see who it was I was momentarily stunned. It was the loser from way back but who had crossed my mind only a few days ago. I recognised him instantly.

"And what do you want?" I asked, raising my eyebrows. He looked at the floor, he was nervous, looked almost frightened as he turned bright red.

"I thought you'd never come back," he spluttered still looking at the floor. "I've been here a dozen times in the last year but you never showed up."

I muttered something about not needing to work so much anymore which was a total lie, but it hit me almost immediately that this man was desperate to hook up with me again. The very fact he'd had the nerve to approach me like that showed how anxious he really was. It had been so long. I remembered the night well though and remembered at the time thinking I'd hit the jackpot finding a man who would pay me to almost abuse him. But then my life had taken a new direction and David had breezed into my world. This was my second chance and I wasn't going to blow it this time.

I looked at him coldly as he squirmed under my glare.

"What the fuck do you want, why are you bothering me?"

I knew why he was here for God sake but I just wanted to hear him say it.

"I can't stop thinking about you Zeta, I mean Mistress Zeta; I needed to see you again."

"You want to see me in VIP?" I asked, slightly taken aback being called Mistress

"Yes Mistress, please."

He was almost salivating. I reached for his tie and pulled it towards me.

"Very well," I said. "You can pay for my time tonight but I'm expensive and I want some information from you."

"Yes of course Mistress, anything you say."

I stood and walked away, I didn't turn around to see if he was following on behind but somehow knew he would be. I walked towards the VIP area and opened the door into the plush velvet den. As I turned around there he was, three feet away.

"Sit the fuck down," I demanded.

He did as he was told.

We sat opposite each other at a small round table and I ordered a bottle of champagne on his tab.

"My time will cost you two hundred and fifty pounds," I said. "There will be no naked flesh and no dancing is that clear?"

He nodded like one of those nodding dogs that sits in the back of a car on the parcel shelf.

"If you tell me what I want to know I may choose to see you again, if not you can take a hike, is that clear?"

"Yes Mistress."

"You are a total loser, do you understand?"

"Yes Mistress."

I tapped the table.

"Show me the colour of your money, NOW!"

He reached into his jacket pocket and counted out ten twenty pound notes from the bundle in his worn leather wallet, then five tens and placed the money on a pile in the middle of the table.

He did it slowly and I could see that he was taking great pleasure in doing so. As each note was positioned upon the table his excitement seemed to heighten.

So here I was on a Tuesday night with two hundred and fifty pounds in front of me at the start of what should have been a long tedious shift. I wanted to know more about this fetish of his, sure I had had guys who wanted to massage my feet or got off on stockings or shoes but this was something different and I wanted to find out more.

"Tell me about what happened last time," I asked him. "Tell me what made you feel the way you did."

He opened up in a big way. He wanted to tell me everything so that I would keep my side of the bargain and allow him to see me again. He went on to describe that when I had stood up to him and defended myself, humiliating him in the process and it had turned him on massively. He looked a little ashamed as he told me about the type of videos he had been watching and jacking off to. He had been doing it for years. Always a domineering foul-mouthed Mistress clad in PVC or leather, or a brazen female boss type, dressed in a smart office suit humiliating an employee, mocking and degrading them.

I could feel myself getting more and more interested in what he was telling me. He said it was a common fetish and that there were chat sites around the world where like-minded men could talk about their own particular type of turn on. He said that when I gave him the finger during my stage routine he had an instant hard on and when he got home he wanked himself stupid. I was dumbstruck, was this really happening to me?

We talked for forty minutes and he confided in me and went on to explain that it wasn't just the verbal abuse but the way the dominatrix acts. He said I was perfect, the best he'd ever seen, superior, aloof with a demeaning character. I was so pleased inside but kept my poker face firmly in place. I made a mental list of everything he was telling me including the websites he was mentioning.

"So tell me the best bit about the evening," I said.

He didn't hesitate; he came back at me immediately.

"I loved giving you my money Mistress; that was the best bit because then I knew you were completely in control of me."

Oh God was I hearing this right? This guy LOVED the fact I took his money? My God! Most of the customers in this place hated handing over money for a dance but this guy was the exact opposite and further more didn't even get a dance!

I looked at my watch; I couldn't believe I'd been talking to him for over an hour.

"Time's up dork," I said.

But the time wasn't up because he begged me for another thirty minutes of abuse as he passed over another one hundred pounds and asked me to degrade and laugh at him.

I stood up, moved closer to him grabbing his collar and looked at his desperate little face.

"'You really are a pathetic excuse for a human being aren't you?"

"Yes, yes I am, I'm so pathetic Mistress I don't even deserve to be in your company."

I leaned closer and sneered at him, notching up my acting to a new level.

"It's a good job you had more money on you, isn't it loser boy?"

"Oh yes Mistress, I wouldn't dream of coming to see you with no money. Everything I earn is yours Mistress."

Holy crap! I wanted to scream, this was getting better and better and I loved what he was telling me. Keep the act up I told myself, poker face Jess, don't give anything away.

I teased him and laughed at him for the rest of our time together and pointed to other customers in the club, telling him that he was not like them, that they were real men. The more I insulted him the more his face told me he was enjoying every minute. When the session eventually grew to a close I told him to, "get the fuck out of here."

He thanked me over and over again and asked permission to come and see me after his next pay day. I told him I'd think about it and as he left he meekly passed me another fifty pounds and said I had made a reality of his fantasy.

As I walked out my mind was in overdrive. Was this my get out of jail card, my chance to leave the club scene forever?

As I walked into the changing rooms the girls eyed me up. They knew it had been the longest I had ever been in the VIP suite with one client and I made sure my money was safely tucked away.

They wanted to know what I had been doing and why it had lasted so long.

I needed to be careful; I didn't want to let my secret slip. I realised a long time ago it was every girl for themselves in club world. It was dog eat dog and the rich clients were at a premium, particularly in these lean times and now I felt I had discovered something a little different that paid well, extremely well and I wanted to keep it to myself, nurture it and turn it into something that might just allow me to turn the corner.

"You obviously did well tonight," one of the new girls said, "judging by the smile on your face. Perhaps you were offering more than a sexy little dance," she sneered sarcastically.

I could feel my blood boil but I had to stay cool.

"Not my style darling," I grinned. "I'll leave that to the desperate little scrubbers like you."

Her face flushed bright red and as some of the other girls started laughing. I simply walked over to my station in front of the mirror and began to take off my 'stripper' makeup. Like I said, it was every girl for themselves in there and I had seen some horrendous squabbles and even fist fights over trivial little things. That said, occasionally there was big money to be made from some clients and they don't come easy. The loser was mine, the easiest money I'd ever earned in the club and I was damned sure I was going to keep him.

By the time I got home I was shattered but also on a bit of a high. The night had proven to be fruitful and full of surprises. I made myself something to eat and wrote a page of notes on a notepad as I sat in bed. I snuggled up next to little Russell and fell asleep.

I awoke at a ridiculously early hour and with a cup of strong black coffee, sat at my laptop. I set to work to find out more of this hidden world.

Within about twenty minutes I got my first break when I stumbled across a website dedicated to Financial Domination. I remembered the loser had said the best part of the evening had been surrendering his money. Jesus Christ, there were more people like him out there. The site was an American site and right at the bottom of the page they were advertising for girls. In for a penny I thought, so I booked in with a photographer I knew the following day and got some moody dominatrix looking pictures done and Mistress Zeta was ready for business. I sent off an email that basically said what a horrible dominating wicked little bitch I was, the shortest CV I had ever put together and within a few hours they got back to me and said they were keen to start me off with a profile.

They asked me to do a slot on webcam once a week where I could set my rate per minute and offer private sessions with the members of the site.

The speed of the way things happened took me by surprise. Not only had I never done webcam before but I was brand new to this whole fetish scene so I was feeling a little nervous. I so nearly bottled it and part of me wanted to email them straight back and tell them I had changed my mind. I was real panicky at the thought of having to sit in front of God knows how many people looking for a real life dominatrix.

Suddenly I had a brainwave, lucky for me the loser was due to come in and see me that week so I could extract a little more information from him and squeeze in a little more practice before going live on line to America. I emailed the company back and said I would get back to them in a few days.

It was Friday night and I danced half-heartedly on stage willing the loser to make an appearance. If only he had known how much I wanted him to show up, he would have died. I knew he would come in and when he did I was pleased to see him but of course I had to keep up the act.

As I finished the dance I walked over to the bar. Sure enough, within twenty seconds he had pulled up a seat next to me.

"What the fuck do you want loser boy?" I said as I waved my hand to get the attention of the barman.

"Well Mistress," he said, "I have a little proposal for you, if you will allow me the chance to explain."

I turned to him casually as I leant up against the rich mahogany bar pulling him towards me with his tie.

"You do realise that if you are about to ask me anything of a sexual nature not only will I heavily fine you, I will throw you to the bouncers and you will no longer have the pleasure of my company ever again."

"Oh God no Mistress," he stuttered, "nothing of the sort, nothing like that Mistress."

He reached for his beer glass and took a long drink before wiping his mouth with his shirt sleeve.

"It's all very innocent, nothing sexual, honest," he blurted out."

I released his tie and he flopped back into his seat.

"Follow me to the VIP lounge," I said, "and make it quick, I haven't got all night and pick up that bill please."

I motioned to the receipt next to my white wine spritzer, spun on my heels and sauntered off leaving him to pay the barman as I headed for VIP. I settled in the corner amongst the plush fabric cushions and watched as the loser almost ran in to meet me. He was positively glowing as he sat down and then proceeded to tell me exactly what it was he wanted me to do with him.

He said one of his fantasies was that I would be his bitch of a girlfriend; a role-play and I would play the girlfriend from hell. Everywhere we went together I had to insult him, no matter where we were, in the street, on the tube, in a bar but particularly in the shops. I had to tell him I was with him only for his money, repeatedly taunt him about how I slept with other men and how much better in bed they were. I had to taunt and tease him loudly so that people could hear and... this was the best bit, I had to do all this while we were out shopping, buying me anything I liked with his credit card!

Oh my God! Was this man serious? I was actually quite speechless as he continued. He wanted to meet me the next day and asked if I was free to act out this long-standing fantasy of his, he said his credit card had a decent limit. I wasn't convinced; surely he was taking the mickey? Surely there was no man on the planet that actually got off on something like this? I thought back to the American Financial Domination site and remembered one man talking about getting his credit card 'maxed' out by his bitch of a girlfriend. I looked at him. He was no longer stuttering like he had done in the past, he was in full flow, animated and grinning broadly as he tried to pin me down to a time.

I wasn't sure what to do at first but the more I thought about it and the more he explained about the details of his fantasy and that we'd be shopping in public the more I realised there was no actual danger involved – it wasn't like I was about to go to a hotel room with anyone or out in a stranger's car in the middle of nowhere. I was going to max out some guy's credit card whilst abusing him in the process. I remember looking at him after he talked for about ten minutes and before I could open my mouth he looked into my eyes and saw the doubt there.

"Oh yes Mistress, I'm deadly serious."

He reached into his wallet and pulled out a wad of notes which he placed on the table, and then he took out a gold Barclays Bank credit card and pushed it on top of the money.

"The cash is for tonight," he said. "Tomorrow I'll punch in my PIN number to any machine you put that into."

I still played hard to get, saying tomorrow was short notice but I could possibly manage it. The truth was I couldn't bloody wait because I believed everything he was saying. Sometimes you sense when a man is talking crap, you can smell it but this certainly wasn't one of those occasions.

We arranged a place and time and discussed it a little more. He asked if I would wear designer shoes, a fitted over the knee skirt and a low cut top and I readily agreed whilst at the same time making sure I was still acting and playing the part of the Mistress.

"Mistress," he said, "you have no idea how long I have wanted this, thank you so much, I'm sure you will enjoy yourself at my expense."

I wanted to tell him he had no idea how long I had waited for a man to say "enjoy yourself at my expense" but of course I couldn't.

So I sneered as I answered him.

"I'm sure I will loser, now run along because I'm sick of the sight of you and don't be late or you'll be fucking sorry."

"Yes Mistress, thank you so much, I really don't deserve you but I promise I'll be waiting for you tomorrow, I won't be a minute late."

Before I even had a chance to say goodbye he'd scuttled off. I wandered back through to the bar and ordered a drink. I didn't dance much more that night, instead I made a mental note of some of the clothes and shoes I'd been looking at over the last twelve months and wondered if my wardrobe was about to take on a designer look.

I looked at my reflection in the mirror before I left for the shopping trip, I was nervous, I would be lying if I said I wasn't. It was different talking to the loser like a bitch down at the club, behind the dim lights and the security of burly doormen, but now I felt a little afraid, vulnerable even.

I was wearing what he had asked me to wear, my long blonde hair was in loose waves down my back and my makeup was quite natural apart from my dark, red pouting lips. I took a deep breath and sighed. Russell who was sitting by my feet looked up and wagged his tail and I took this as positive feedback! I gave him a hug and a kiss, grabbed my large Louis Vuitton handbag and a heavy tweed coat which would keep out the cold wind and left the house.

I parked in the city centre car park and with one last look in the car mirror I headed off to the meeting point, giving myself a silent pep talk as I walked, trying to control my breathing.

He was there waiting for me. I wanted to give him a little kiss on the cheek or a hug but of course I couldn't. I sauntered over to him as I looked him up and down.

"Mistress, I'm so glad you came."

I turned my nose up.

"Whatever loser, you know why I'm here, don't you?"

"Yes and I can't wait for you to spend all my money," he beamed.

I was dreaming surely? How surreal I chuckled to myself, how many girls would love to hear those words? He told me again that we were playing a boyfriend girlfriend role and I was to call him John. He wanted a name from me and I told him to still continue calling me Zeta. I was an actress and using the name Zeta and not Jess gave me the confidence I needed. John wanted every man's fantasy, he wanted an attractive haughty blonde on his arm, someone expensive and with taste, something he knew he would never get in the real world, but John wanted more, he wanted full on public humiliation.

We were sorted. It was time to act.

"Follow me loser," I said. "Let's start in the beauty department of John Lewis, the new guy I'm screwing just loves my Chanel fragrance and I'm about to run out."

His mouth fell open but his eyes were dancing, his fantasy was about to become reality.

I acted the part of the perfect bitch swanning around the huge department store before making my way up to the cosmetics on the first floor as the loser followed on behind. We stood in front of the shop assistant and he took his role well as he picked up a small bottle of Chanel Coco.

"This one's nice dear," he said.

I looked at the shop assistant and then back to him with a look of disgust on my face.

"What the hell are you talking about?" I said. "What the fuck would you know you hopeless creature," I spat in a whisper.

The shop assistant nearly fell over as John lowered his head. I looked at the assistant.

"Chanel No 5 please. What size do you have and don't worry about the price because my useless boyfriend is paying."

It was the assistant's lucky day as she quickly loaded several boxes onto the counter and I started to browse. I talked about him to the assistant all the while as if he wasn't there. I said what a useless specimen he was and how shit he was in bed and that I was only with him because of his money. The poor girl was gobsmacked as she avoided eye contact with him throughout the exchange. I selected a 100ml bottle of perfume and a velvet body lotion; the total cost came to two hundred and seven pounds.

I handed the girl his credit card and watched as she inserted it into the card machine and he punched in his pin number. I half expected the card to be rejected but it was fine. As she removed his card and handed it across towards him I swiftly grabbed it from her.

"Don't think I've finished with that," I sneered at him. "I haven't even fucking started."

It was a nice sale for the girl but I think she was glad to see the back of us. I continued the charade in John Lewis for about an hour and I swear their departmental phones were ringing red-hot. I clocked up over £700 worth of sales and then we headed outside. I needed some new kit for the gym so I directed him to one of the more upmarket sports outlets where he bought me two pairs of Adidas trainers and a top of the range running attire. I started talking about my affairs in front of the young male shop assistant and at one point flirted outrageously with him. The poor bastard didn't know where to look as I announced that I was in dire need of some hot sex.

Two hours later and laden with shopping bags the loser was hanging on my every word, asking me who I was having affairs with and where these men were taking me on dates, I played my part in his fantasy role play just about perfectly, if I say so myself and was being rewarded handsomely for it.

"I want some lunch," I announced, "and when we're eating I'll tell you all about these dirty little sex sessions I've been having behind your back."

"Yes Zeta."

We went to a high-end sushi bar and as we settled down to a bottle of champagne I started to tease him in front of the waiters. I said that my new lover was a real man who knew exactly how to please me and I'd had more orgasms with him than any other previous lover I'd had and if he had been a little richer I'd have no hesitation in walking out on our relationship.

He was begging me to stop but I went on and on saying my new lover had the biggest cock I'd ever seen.

"Please don't leave me," he begged, "I'll do anything Zeta, anything."

"Okay," I said, "Go and jack off in the toilets now," I demanded.

He was momentarily stunned. "What? Oh God oh I..." he stammered going bright red.

"Go to the toilets now," I repeated, "and wank off you useless cretin because that's the only action you're going to get today."

He nodded slowly as he climbed from his seat.

"I'll be waiting," I teased him and off he scuttled, looking over his shoulder several times until he reached the toilets.

Approximately three minutes later he surfaced from the gents looking slightly red in the face, but obviously satisfied. I laughed out loud as I stood up to put my coat on as he returned to the table.

"Mistress, thank you, that was an amazing day, we should do it again soon."

I was trying hard to stay in the role. I wanted to thank him for the presents he had bought me and I wanted to thank him for a strangely different day and for giving me ideas and a way out of my daily monotony. I looked down at the Jimmy Choo bags, the Chanel gift box among my many treats from the day and tried to keep my composure.

But in the end I did break the act as I told him I had enjoyed making his fantasy somewhat of a reality. I jotted down my email address and said he should contact me direct if he wanted to do it again.

He looked bowled over, like the cat that got the cream. Before he could say another word I told him I should get going.

As he walked away through the door I ordered another glass of champagne and decided I could take a taxi home.

Chapter Five

My first day on webcam for the American site was kind of funny and in a way it was a relief to find that not only did I find it fun but it didn't freak me out either. Don't get me wrong I was a bloody nervous wreck because this was real acting; acting on a little screen and in front of people I couldn't see, only hear. It was so different because when I'd been playing the part at the club or in the real-time shopping trip I could see the client and always felt in control. I had a large glass of wine prior to the first time I went live in the States. I leaned over the computer and pressed the stream live button and didn't have a clue how I would react to my first invisible submissive. The man was called Don and he was from Oregon. I remember being a little disappointed at the money at first. I was paid no more than twenty five pounds for the first time but as I abused and shouted and ridiculed Don from Oregon I could sense he was on a short fuse and he wasn't going to last long. He didn't. At precisely twenty one minutes in I could hear him breathing heavily and at twenty two minutes I ordered him to get his member into his hand and he obeyed without question. I squirmed a little as I heard him perform and at twenty four minutes it was all over. He thanked me and just as I was about to abuse him some more the connection ended and he was gone. I checked my account on line; the money was there, just over twenty-five quid for the twenty five minutes. I checked the screen and my inbox and there was another client waiting for me if I wanted to indulge him.

I think at this point in time I realised the potential of this strange but lucrative business concept. I was working from home, choosing my own hours and I was making around fifty pounds an hour. There were no office or travel expenses and even when I declared my earnings to the tax man, which I always did, it was far better money for example than an area managers secretary in the city centre where I lived. This wasn't bad at all and furthermore there seemed to be an ever-growing supply of clients who were only too keen to book in a slot with the abusive Mistress Zeta. The time difference in the US meant I had to plan my diary accordingly but although there were some unsociable hours it wasn't impossible by any stretch of the imagination.

And as my client bank grew and I started to gain a reputation I actually began to enjoy my sessions. Not once was I subject to any abuse from the other end or ever messed around. I made sure the money was always in my account before I started and I think that got rid of the timewasters.

I was fulfilling a service and as crazy as this may seem, at times I felt like a mix between a psychiatrist and a village GP. I've always been a people person and like to help people feel at ease, this was no different right? These men were pouring their hearts out to me, as if they trusted me like their best friend and felt fully at ease describing the most fucked up fantasies and deepest desires you could ever think of in the hope that I could satisfy them but also make them feel that they weren't fucked up after all. Believe me there were times I wanted to burst out laughing and say, "You want me to do what?"

But of course you can't or word would filter back and the money tap would be turned off. I realised fairly quickly that I could cope with this profession and yes, I was fulfilling a service that most of society would ridicule.

The clients asked the question quite often

"Do you think I am strange or fucked up, a pervert or warped?"

I would answer in my role that of course they were fucked up but then I would continue to order them to do what it was I wanted, so the fact I was encouraging them to continue their fantasy meant that I sort of approved so therefore I didn't believe they were fucked up at all. Does that make sense?

Whatever. It worked because under your profile is a button that each client can activate and leave a genuine comment on how each dominatrix performed. Well, not one to boast but within a few months my profile was getting more hits than anyone on the site and I was on a 94% rating with five star recommendations all over the place and comments like;

"Mistress Zeta gives the best sessions possible." "Mistress is GREAT at what she does, the best dom I've come across." "Mistress indulges your fantasies, so you really enjoy your time with her."

You get the picture, it's like an Amazon book review site and if the buyers like what they see then they buy. Before long I was running a fourteen hour a day diary and I was getting tired and the work (after a fourteen hour day) was getting a little tedious.

I was getting more and more requests for real time sessions but of course it was impossible because all of the clients were in America. I posted on the site that I was living in the United Kingdom so real time sessions were out of the question but one man from Texas said he would pay for my flights and accommodation if I promised him three real time sessions on alternate days. I emailed him—'You've got to be joking'.

He wasn't. He said the money for the flights would be in my account as soon as I agreed, hotel booked in advance and a $5000 cheque waiting for me on arrival. I was sorely tempted until I Googled the flight times and duration. Texas was on the other side of the world as far as I was concerned, surely there were clients a little nearer to home?

So I updated my profile, said I lived near to London and set a rate of three hundred and fifty pounds per hour, four star plus hotels only and made my mind up that I would agree my first client before the end of the week as long as I felt happy about the fetish they had.

The following night I had a message on the site from a man in Ilford.

> "Hello Mistress, my long time fantasy has been for my owner to dress me up in a slutty French maid outfit and make me serve her champagne. I also dream of being locked in a chastity belt while I cater to her every need."

He went on to describe how he would wear a blonde wig and stockings and suspender with stilettos along with the exact shade of lipstick he wanted to wear for me. I stared at the information in front of me. Shall I? How bad could this be? It actually looked like fun, watching a sissy fussing around me donned in full maid attire in a hotel of my choice.

I teased him over several emails and managed to get the price up by another one hundred pounds. Finally I agreed a meeting in a well-known hotel near to where I lived.

I told him the session would last an hour, no more, I would arrive first, go up to the room and call him in the bar with the room number. He was to bring everything including the props. What's a French maid without a feather duster? He didn't ask me to wear anything in particular, just said I was to look high class and very powerful. I opted for a black tight skirt, a black and cream peplum top showing plenty of cleavage and a new pair of patent leather five inch stilettos and my old faithful oversized Louis Vuitton bag. My 'look' was just about complete and a couple of hours before I met up with 'Tom' I visited the hairdressers and had my hair put into a sleek, wavy high pony tail with clip in extensions. I decided on what was becoming the trademark look of big pouty red lips. As I walked through towards the hotel reception through the lobby I noticed my reflection in a full length mirror. I was pleased with the look and was aware of one or two stares but how I was dressed filled me with much needed confidence in my hour of need. I checked in and went up to the room, ordered champagne and after fifteen minutes called my client.

Within five minutes there was a knock at the door. I took a deep breath and walked over towards the door and opened it. Shit! His size almost blocked out the light, a big burly guy with a large holdall. His reaction in seeing me gave nothing away, his face was emotionless and suddenly I was nervous, and yes, a little frightened. Was he really here for what he said he was here for? He didn't look like a submissive but then again what do they look like? At that particular point in time I wondered if he was about to push me into the hotel room and attack me. What the hell had I got myself into, I was starting to panic! What was I doing here? What sort of business had I got involved in? Before I could give the matter any thought, he breezed past me and walked into the room, turned to face me and smiled.

I needed to take control of the situation and play out the role he allegedly wanted me to play. I'd know soon enough if he was genuine.

"Go and change," I said forcefully. I pointed towards the bathroom. "Immediately, I haven't got all fucking day."

"Yes of course Mistress," he replied.

I breathed out deeply and began to relax a little hearing this submissive, soft voiced reply.

"I may be a while Mistress I want to look perfect when I serve you"

I smiled. "Run along my little sissy, Mistress will be waiting for you."

I motioned towards the bathroom and walked past him to sit on the large bed. He disappeared into the bathroom and I took out a handkerchief and wiped my hot brow. I was feeling a little better but still felt a little shaky and wished he'd left the bathroom door open so that I could see what he was doing.

He was in there for about fifteen minutes but it felt like an hour. As he opened the door and stepped back into the bedroom my relief was immeasurable as he stood nervously, dressed exactly as he said he would be in the email, all six and a half feet of him. His high stiletto, stripper heels took his height to around seven foot and the top of his head was dangerously close to the ceiling. He looked utterly ridiculous and it took all of my willpower to keep my composure. His black stockings weren't quite long enough, and the suspender belt strained under the pressure. His leg hair was clearly visible through the material and it was like something from an old Carry On comedy movie. The French maid's outfit was cheap looking and his blonde Marilyn Monroe wig straight from the local fancy dress shop. His make-up was a disaster area, overly done red cheeks paired with messy eyeliner and finished off with red rosy lipstick and feather duster held aloft. The poor bastard looked positively petrified.

I stood and walked over to him. I was like a dwarf looking up to a giant.

"Well what do we have here?" I said. "A pretty little sissy all to myself?"

He appeared to relax as he smiled apprehensively.

"Yes Mistress," he said shyly, "it's all for you."

I looked him up and down slowly, giving his blouse a playful tug.

"Give me a twirl then my dear; show me the full naughty outfit."

He looked me in the eye and spoke.

"Please Mistress, call me Marilyn."

I nearly collapsed on the bed. This acting was harder than I had ever thought, I was surely in the running for an Oscar as I bit my lip and spoke.

"Of course, Marilyn, why don't you give me a twirl?"

He obeyed meekly as he beamed a broad grin, gave me a full twirl followed by a delicate curtsey.

I leaned forward and reached for the hem of his tiny skirt lifting it slowly. I told him to take down his frilly panties and he did so.

"Well, well," I said as I observed his flaccid cock hanging limply from his chastity contraption, a small wire cage fitted with a tiny brass padlock.

"Give me the key," I said. "I'm in control here."

He reached into his breast pocket and handed me the key

"Good girl," I said, "pull them back up."

"Yes Mistress."

"Now see the room service trolley over there?"

"Yes Mistress."

"Be a good sissy and get me a glass of champagne."

"Yes Mistress."

He wheeled the trolley over as I lay back on the super king size bed remembering what it was he said he'd wanted to do for me in his e-mails. He slowly and carefully opened the bottle, cleaned the glass with a handkerchief and poured then handed me a glass. I took a large mouthful; I was at ease now and didn't feel he posed a threat of any sort.

"Remove my shoes, and be careful," I said.

"Yes Mistress, of course Mistress."

"Now," I said, "Mistress wants to relax. What do you think makes Mistress relax best of all?"

"Oh please let me give you a foot rub Mistress," he said.

I was actually looking forward to this bit because it had been a particular long shift at the club, seven bloody hours and my feet were killing me. I couldn't wait for his big strong hands massaging my little tired feet.

"Yes, do that, my feet are tired and sore."

So I lay on the bed perfectly relaxed as he produced a bottle of scented body oil and began to massage my feet. I stopped him every few minutes so that I could take I sip of bubbly.

After he had finished he soaped and rinsed my feet then dried them. He stood in the corner of the room and asked what was required next. He passed me a magazine and I read for a while as he stood quietly in the corner of the room. He changed the TV channels when I asked him and finally I had him dust every corner and every surface of the room and then he poured me another glass of champagne.

Marilyn tended to my every whim and I was paid four hundred and fifty pounds for little over an hour. He paid for the room and the champagne and as I looked at my watch and realised it was nearly time I beckoned him forward and ordered him to lift his skirt and take off his panties.

His poor cock was straining under the pressure and I was well aware that if it hadn't been so restricted it would have been standing up as stiff as a poker.

I held the glass of champagne to my mouth.

"Now Marilyn, you know what I want you to do next?"

"Yes Mistress."

I threw him the key and he unlocked the padlock and removed his chastity cage. His cock sprung into life and he immediately went to take hold of himself.

"No!" I shouted at him angrily. "Only when I say."

"Sorry Mistress."

I let him stew for a few minutes before I allowed him to pleasure himself.

"Okay," I said, "wank off into your little frilly knickers for Mistress."

He couldn't wait as he took a hold of his cock and began beating away at himself. His hand was a blur as I continued to read a magazine, sipping my champagne. Within a couple of minutes he let out a loud groan and filled his knickers as he ejaculated.

"Get into the bathroom you filthy little bitch and clean yourself up."

"Yes Mistress."

Fifteen minutes later he came back out in his jeans and polo shirt as if the events of the last hour had never happened. He gave me the money as if he'd just paid for a personal training session; it was all rather bizarre as he talked about the weather and his journey back home in the car.

"Thank you so much," he said. "You have no idea how long I have waited to do that, thank you so much and thank you for not laughing at me."

That last sentence tugged at the old heart strings I have to admit, because it would have been so easy to find the humour and yet I knew if I had laughed at him it would have ruined the pleasure he undoubtedly took from our hour together.

"Thank you for a lovely afternoon," he said.

"I'm very glad you enjoyed it," I said. "We must do it again."

His face lit up.

"Really? You really mean that?"

I wanted to take his two cheeks in my hands and plant a big kiss on his lips and tell him how much I had enjoyed the session and of course the ridiculous fee but I remained composed.

"Yes, you were very attentive; you can call me in a week or two."

We parted ways and I headed to a nearby coffee shop for some lunch and took stock of what had just happened. Not only had it been fun, financially it was a way out of the club scene and I most certainly wanted to do it again. But I was more than aware how frightened I had felt initially. There was no way around that when meeting with new clients who were total strangers. Suddenly as I thought about finding another new client along the same lines as Marilyn, the fear factor was returning.

Chapter Six

For the first time since I'd walked out on David I was able to put a little bit of money to one side. I was in control again and although I had to work long hours on the American website I was in control of my own destiny. But in the back of my mind I knew if I could take hold of this new area of income and channel my efforts in the right direction I could make a fortune. The only trouble was my own state of mind. I wanted to find more Marilyns and fill my diary and not bother with the club but of course the club offered security, I felt safe there and although I was growing tired of the work I couldn't shake that awful moment from my mind, when I had stood alone and vulnerable in the doorway of a strange hotel room staring out onto the Incredible Hulk.

I sat at the computer on a wet Sunday evening staring at the screen in between watching the raindrops racing each other down the window pane. There were two more requests in my area for real time sessions. I wanted to open them and consider a reply but instead I minimised the whole site and logged onto Outlook to check my emails that had come in over the weekend and wondered what it was that was holding me back.

I walked into the club the following Monday evening. I must have looked a little miserable as one of the bouncers and the barmaid both passed a comment. The club was quiet that night, full of guys with little or no money taking in the sights and drinking the beer on the two for one special. I looked around to see if the loser had showed up but couldn't see him anywhere.

An old friend of mine from a club I used to work at had telephoned me and said she was making an appearance around midnight and I looked forward to catching up on some gossip. When she arrived and we got talking she said the old club had taken a turn for the worse and the management had wanted to up the house fee for dancing there. For those of you who are unfamiliar with the business, the dancers work without a regular salary, that is, the clubs don't pay their dancers, we pay them and simply keep what we earn. The club also wanted to take on more dancers so the alarm bells were ringing loudly telling us that all was not well.

As soon as I got talking to Anna I sensed something wasn't quite right. She looked harder, her face a little worn if that makes sense and I noticed some scars that hadn't been there the last time I'd met up with her.

The tears welled up in her eyes (and mine) as I found out Anna had got involved with some guy who I had seen from time to time, meeting with the management of the old club. He was a mean looking guy with tattoos on his face and built like a brick shit house, it was rumoured that he took protection money from the management to 'look after' the place. We had all been warned to stay away from him but it transpired Anna hadn't heeded the warning and started buying a gram or two of cocaine from him. Anna explained that she had always felt in control of her social habit but as always, it had taken a hold of her and she suddenly realised that she was shovelling more powder up her nose than her income could support.

Mr Gangster Man was very understanding and quite sweet at first. He had taken Anna out after the club and wined and dined her in London's finest, supplying her with enough coke to fill a large bucket. Anna thought the arrangement suited her fine at first and knew she was expected to jump into bed with her dealer whenever he desired. A kind attentive lover at first, though occasionally a little too aggressive for her liking she said. Anna was crying as she explained the arrangement took a turn for the worse after about six weeks. He'd wanted her to go a little further and join him in a threesome with another girl who worked at the club. Anna had flatly refused so he drove her back to her apartment as they hardly said a word. He walked with her to the apartment door and as she opened the door he pushed her inside and attacked her smashing her face to bits. As he stood over her broken body he laid the law down and said that she had overstepped the line. She worked for him now, she was effectively his property as he explained she would need to work long and hard as her cocaine invoice now stood at over seven grand.

My stomach flipped as I learned that this feisty Thai girl who I used to have such fun with on an occasional night out was now a full blown coke addict and a shadow of her former self. She had resorted to servicing the management of the old club in a desperate attempt to try and lower her bill with the man who now controlled her. She smiled, she actually smiled as she told me she'd managed to get her debt with him down to less than five thousand and by the end of the year she might be clear of him all together, but of course I knew that would never happen.

He cleared a hundred pounds a time, she explained, if she serviced him or any of his associates. She looked a little sheepish as she told me that one evening he'd demanded she turn up at a stag do in a private room in one of the rougher joints in London's East End. She had been the evening's entertainment that night as she was forced to have sex with the half drunk groom, the best man and the ushers in a five man group sex party. Anna smiled proudly as she said she'd cleared seven hundred pounds from the debt for one nights work but had got a little carried away when she'd accepted 'one or two lines' at the end of the night.

I could have cried for poor Anna, she would never ever clear that debt, not that she knew it, because once men like that get their claws into vulnerable girls they never let them go. They picked on the weak; they singled out the girls who had messed up lives and serious issues or those naïve little lambs who knew no better.

Anna left, she was due on stage and as I sat alone near the bar I looked around the club taking everything in. I didn't belong here. The girls were either weak or hardened to the scene, it appeared there was nothing in between. They wore fake smiles, along with the false lashes and rub on tan and they either acted the part well or cried out for help and those that did were exploited by the men who could spot them from a country mile. It was a terrible scene, a den of iniquity and I no longer wanted to be part of it. I couldn't help but think of the friends I knew that had lost their way, girls who drifted on to other clubs more downmarket or into prostitution.

I am never one to judge – how can you when each individual has their own story, a troubled background, their own heart-breaking tale? Anna was seriously into cocaine and paying for her habit by sleeping with upwards of twenty men a week. I wanted to help her, I wanted to tell her she needed help but when she came off stage and I talked with her again I could see she was in a hopeless zombie-like trance with only one consideration and that was where her next line would be coming from. There was nothing else that mattered. She wasn't interested in her apartment or what she was having for dinner and she'd forgotten her family's birthdays and anniversaries a long time ago. That was just as well because she was now an embarrassment to them all. Her sister she'd once spoken so proudly of had sent one unanswered text too many and her boyfriend of five years had walked out just after Christmas last year when she'd failed to show up at the annual Christmas dinner. She'd been seeing to Gangster Man in the back of his Range Rover at the time they'd served the main course.

I stayed on at the club for the rest of the week. I studied the girls, many of them I classed as good friends and it all became apparent what we were doing to ourselves. We all thought it was easy money, a little dancing and cash in the hand. It wasn't, it was like riding the 'disaster express' and the inevitable crash would happen sooner or later but it would happen.

I pitied the younger, newer girls coming in thinking it was easy, not knowing the consequences of working in a dark world like this and thinking they could handle it. I had been like that too once upon a time but I had seen the light and was getting out relatively unscathed.

On the final night I watched them as they stood in front of groups of men pleading for a twenty pound dance, how degrading can you get? The men laughed and hurled insults and pointed out innocuous flaws, while the girls laughed and teased and flirted.

I was in no mood to dance and I asked the manager if I could leave a little early, claiming I'd been feeling ill all night and he reluctantly agreed.

I desperately needed a drink and a chat with someone so as I left the club I phoned Ella, my best friend from the club scene. Ella worked up the west end and always finished earlier than the rest of the girls. She answered her phone in a whisper but nevertheless I could tell she was pleased to hear from me.

"Why are you whispering?" I asked. "Have you finished for the night?'

"'No babe," she said, "but I've left the club, I'm... I'm with a customer having a few drinks."

"Well, where are you?" I demanded, "I'm in desperate need of some company, I need to talk."

I explained briefly that I was thinking of leaving the club and wanted to try something else but I sensed almost immediately that she wasn't listening, or worse, wasn't interested in what it was I was saying.

"What is it Ella?" I said. "You're not even interested are you?"

Ella apologised, admitted she hadn't been listening and said it would have to wait until another night.

"Fuck that," I said, "he's just a customer and anyway you know the rules Ella, you shouldn't be with a customer outside of club hours. Tell him to sling his hook and I'll be wherever you want me to be."

Ella gave a nervous laugh, said that I needed to get into the real world occasionally.

"I'm in his hotel room," she said. "He's booked me for the next two hours."

"Ella!" I yelled, "what the hell? What do you mean at his hotel, you're screwing him?"

Ella was trying to calm me down.

"He's my regular babe, don't worry, listen I have to go I'll call you tomorrow."

"Ella... wait..." I shouted but it was too late, she was gone.

The rest of the drive was a blur. I couldn't quite believe it. Ella was someone I had looked up to, admired. I thought she was one of the strongest girls I had known and I couldn't quite believe she'd turned to this type of entertaining. It was all downhill for her from now on and I knew it. First the Anna bombshell and now Ella too. As I climbed into bed with little Russell I realised just how screwed up the whole scene was and I wanted out. As I lay and stared at the darkened ceiling I made a pledge that I'd never show my face in the club again.

I phoned the manager the following week. He wasn't happy at first and threw the loyalty card in my face, saying that I owed him at least a month's notice in order that he could replace me with someone decent. What a bloody joke, what a liberty. The bastard had grown ridiculously rich by simply allowing vulnerable girls to dance in his premises, paying him for the privilege. I thought about spinning him a yarn about an illness or the death of a relative as he bleated on about how good he had been to me and how he had looked after my interests.

"Roy," I said, "you're a decent bloke but I don't owe you anything, you don't even pay my National Insurance, you've bought me an odd drink over the years but that's about the size of it."

"Jessica," he said, "get your arse down here tonight and at least give me a few weeks to sort something out. You owe it to me."

"Roy," I said, "fuck you and fuck your club."

And with that I pressed the end button on my mobile phone. He rang back within minutes but I cut him off immediately. By the time the hour was out he would get the message.

I took a few days out and walked the legs off poor Russell. He thought it was fantastic as we strolled through the local parks and woodland for hours at a time. It was nice thinking time and I always left my mobile phone behind as I planned my business strategy over the coming months.

I had two regular 'face to face' clients in the loser and Marilyn and between them they just about covered the mortgage. I had the added bonus of never having to fund my own wardrobe as the loser booked me at least once a month and my online American work was building nicely. And yet I was very well aware that the real money was in real time sessions and the big fees would be found in finding the cash fetish clients similar to the loser.

I was finding out more and more about that side of the business and knew they were out there. I was getting the requests but most of them seemed to be based in the US. I just needed to be patient and in all honesty was feeling more confident in myself and the business and felt refreshingly in control of my own destiny. I was laughing a lot more and being far more sociable and went out with friends a lot. I talked and flirted with guys, and was more than aware I still had a sexual drive that needed to be satisfied but I just hadn't met anyone who I wanted to get to know, let alone spend the night with. I had even thought about calling Mark just to hook up with him but the more I thought about it the more I realised I didn't want to get it started again. It was water under the bridge. I made my mind up and came to the conclusion it would happen when it happened.

It's strange working in this industry, satisfying clients' needs on a daily basis and having no one to satisfy your own. Sure I had the toys and believe me the sex toys these days work but there's nothing like the real thing, the body contact, the sensual touch, kissing and reaching a climax together. There is something incredibly fulfilling satisfying your own sexual urges and at the same time doing the same for a person you are very fond of.

But it wasn't to be, not at the present time anyway. I threw myself into the emails from the US site, dozens of them every day and sifted through them, casting most into the recycling bin and offering brief Skype sessions to a selected few. But I was looking for the 'real time' sessions and answered the ones that interested me and prayed that they would be mailing me from England, hopefully within an hour or two's drive from London.

I was frustrated but realised I had to take more Skype sessions to make ends meet, especially from the US as they were coming in thick and fast and on the whole were prepared to pay a little more than their British counterparts. But I was obsessive about keeping my identity secret and was meticulously careful. Okay they could see me, I couldn't do anything about that, but as soon as they started to pry into my real world they were history, blocked and forgotten. It was amazing how many actually asked the question. "What's your real name then Zeta?"

That was the last they'd ever hear from me.

One email took my eye, it was from a man who called himself The Sandwich Man, he was from Savannah in Georgia and wrote a long articulate email about a fetish he said I had likely never come across. The rate he was offering was more than generous and as I neared the end of his mail I nearly fell off my seat as he said all he wanted from me was to make him eat sandwiches. "What on earth?" I mumbled out loud.

I felt in a devilish mood so I replied to him. I called him a depraved loser and went along with his little game saying that if I got involved I would force him to eat more sandwiches than he had ever eaten in his life and I wouldn't stop until he was physically sick.

He replied. It was short and sweet. He said that I was exactly what he was looking for.

My reply was to the point. "When loser?"

His next email was a little longer and more precise giving me specific instructions and a time. He said he wanted me to wear a basque and stockings and suspenders (panty hose in the US) and I was to be forceful and carry the role play through to the end no matter how much he begged me to stop. The end as he described it would be him climaxing on screen; he wanted a dual camera session. I am happy to do dual camera sessions and to be honest if I see something I don't like I have trained myself to look over the computer so that I can't see the subject. As it happened, The Sandwich Man's fetish was so bizarre and warped that I wouldn't be able to tear my eyes away from the screen even if I wanted to.

I took my time getting ready for this one as I somehow sensed it would cross boundaries I never knew existed. I showered and dressed and applied a scandalous shade of scarlet lipstick and tied my hair back from my face. My mascara was over the top as was my rouge but as I turned to look in the mirror I smiled as I thought this was just the sort of look the Sandwich Man was looking for.

Time to wipe the smile from my face I thought, as I was definitely playing the part of a hard faced domineering bitch and laughing and joking was not on the agenda.

I looked at my watch. Five minutes to go. I sat down at the desk and booted up the laptop and positioned and focused the camera.

At precisely ten thirty that evening the Skype display lit up and asked me if I wanted to accept or decline a call from 'Chris from Savannah'.

I pressed accept and stood adopting a forceful pose with both hands on my hips as I glared at the screen. Chris was sitting at his computer and his whole face filled the screen. He smiled.

"Hi," he said. "You look nice Zeta."

I remained cool and aloof and stony silent.

He was immediately on the back foot as he hesitated and started stuttering.

"You've dressed as I asked Zeta, does that mean you will help me?"

I waited twenty or thirty seconds and I could see him almost cringing with discomfort and then I spoke.

"You have the sandwiches ready?"

"Yes Miss."

And then the fun began and I promise you, my dear reader, that everything I am about to describe happened exactly that way. I haven't exaggerated nor have I used any poetic licence. I swear, that this is exactly the fantasy I played out with Chris from Savannah, though I have changed his name to protect his privacy.

Chris was quite handsome, mid-forties but he had looked after himself. I had been expecting a balding bespectacled fat guy but he looked a little like Michael Douglas in his younger days and he had quite a cute smile. What progressed over the next twenty minutes however was anything but cute.

Chris stood and asked me to wait a second or two. He fiddled with the camera and repositioned it so that it now focused on a table and a chair. Sure enough, on top of the table there were three plates piled high with sandwiches. There were about ten sandwiches on each plate. A few seconds later Chris appeared and sat on the seat with an expectant look on his face.

"Okay," I said. "Tell me what sandwiches you have there."

Chris looked over at the plates (as if he didn't know) "Errr... there are some ham ones, cheese and a plate of egg mayo."

Shit! I remembered I hadn't eaten since lunchtime and that was just a small tuna salad. Those sandwiches looked good, I was feeling quite hungry. However what Chris was about to show me would soon quell my appetite.

"Three egg mayo," I barked. "Eat them now."

"Yes Miss."

Chris reached over to one of the plates and lifted three sandwiches off and proceeded to eat them. So far so good and I reminded myself that Chris was paying two hundred dollars for his thirty minute session. I said nothing as he munched away slowly on his three sandwiches. He cleared his mouth of the last piece, swallowed and smiled at the camera. It was time to boost it up a notch or two.

"You stupid idiot, can't you eat them any quicker than that you hopeless piece of shit?" I lingered on my watch. "Do you think I've got nothing better to do?"

He was full of it gushing out his apologies.

"I'm sorry Mistress, I'll do my best for you I promise I will."

I gave him a few more seconds while he squirmed in his seat before I sighed and told him to continue.

"Cheese this time. Four of them and you've got two minutes you fucking loser or I'm calling it a day."

He didn't even answer me as the first of his four cheese sandwiches was stuffed into his mouth. With the first three egg mayo he chewed politely as if he was having afternoon tea at the Ritz but this time he didn't stand on ceremony and I got a bird's eye view of everything he swallowed as my appetite diminished rapidly.

As he crammed the last piece of bread into his mouth I demanded two more cheese and he quickly obliged and at the same time his left hand moved down to his groin for the first time. If I hadn't seen it with my own eyes I would never have believed it. Here was a man getting turned on by eating sandwiches. I'm not particularly religious but for those of you who are I would beg the question: where did your own particular God go wrong in designing a man like this? I was aware that I was staring at the screen and more than likely my mouth gaping open as I watched this incredible spectacle. I quickly jumped back into my role as I realised his mouth was empty now and he was awaiting further instructions.

"The rest of the egg mayo. Now!"

"But Miss can't I have a rest?" he pleaded.

"Can you hell," I said. "Eat them now, all of them and don't stop until you're fucking finished."

He did exactly as I commanded as his right hand reached for the sandwiches and his left hand worked on his cock, which by now had been released from the constraints of his trousers.

But even though he was slowly pleasuring himself, I could now see that he was becoming visibly uncomfortable and no wonder, because by my calculations he had just pushed seventeen sandwiches into his mouth. He had unloosened his belt to his trousers, pushed them down to his knees and stripped his shirt off. I could see his stomach expanding by the second as I bellowed at him to keep eating.

"Please Miss... no more... please."

"Cheese sandwich, you waste of space, two of them."

"Yes Mistress."

"Faster, you hopeless cretin and stop complaining."

I would never have believed it if I hadn't seen it with my own eyes. Surely he couldn't take any more? By now his right hand had slowed down but the speed of his left hand had increased dramatically as I ordered him to eat even more.

"Please Miss I'm going to be sick, I don't want any more."

I changed tact. I don't know why but now I was beginning to sympathise with the depraved bastard, convinced his stomach was just about to split open right in front of me.

"One more for the Mistress."

A slight grin flicked across his face as he started pumping furiously with his left hand as he forced yet another sandwich into his mouth. All of a sudden a greenish hue washed over his face and his head started jerking back and forward as his body went into spasms. I knew exactly what was happening and yet still he forced the final piece of bread into his mouth and down his throat. That last piece of bread had a reunion with at least a litre of vomit as it projected up his throat and out of his mouth in a scene reminiscent of the Exorcist. At exactly the same time I watched in horror as he groaned out loud as an impressive amount of white liquid ejected from the end of his cock and met with the vomit in mid-air. It was quite the most disgusting thing I had ever seen in my life as I realised exactly what it was that this creature got off on. Where the hell had that fantasy originated from?

I stood in stunned silence as he milked every last drop of semen from his dick into the pool of vomit onto the floor. I was retching myself as an acidy bile made its way involuntarily into my mouth.

"You disgusting, vile human being." I shouted at him. This time I wasn't acting. I meant every word.

He looked up with a sick, satisfied, contented grin. "Thank you Mistress, thank you so much," he said.

I rushed over to the laptop and disconnected the call immediately. The dirty, horrible bastard. I almost sprinted as I ran to the bathroom quickly placing my mouth under the tap guzzling as much water as possible. I was breathing heavily and perspiring, all the time wondering what sort of specimen I had unearthed. What the fuck is wrong with these people? Isn't sex simply the greatest sensation you've ever experienced? And while I could understand a little dominatrix role play I just couldn't get my head around what I had just witnessed, it was like something out of a horror movie.

I didn't want it to get to me and yet it did, it was a whole new playing field, how many more 'sandwich men' were out there? At first I had looked on it as a harmless bit of fun, something to laugh at and tell my girlfriends about but the throwing up on the point of orgasm to me, was just gross. I would never share this with any of my girlfriends, I was too ashamed.

It took maybe a day or two to begin working again. When Chris's money hit my account I told myself to get a grip. The money was good; the hourly rate was great because not everyone was cut out for this sort of work. It was inevitable that I would stumble upon an occasional crank because that was the nature of the beast.

I took a trip into town and spent a little of my ill-gotten gains to cheer myself up. As I walked past the local supermarket I looked in the window and saw a job advertised for seven pounds twenty five pence an hour. I smiled to myself. If it was easy everyone would become an online dominatrix. It wasn't easy, I knew that much. I was more than a little special and I could handle the rough with the smooth I told myself.

Chapter Seven

Towards the end of the week I looked at the heading of an email which simply stated – 'forced intoxication and wallet rape'. It sounded very interesting and I loved the sound of the wallet rape so I read on. My jaw hit the floor as the mailer detailed that he wanted to meet me for a real time session and take me out for the day. My role was to get him drunk and then take advantage of his wallet and rid him of a good amount of cash. However much I managed to take from him would be my fee to keep and I nearly fell off my seat when he said it would be in excess of a four figure sum. I typed fast, praying silently that he would be English and live quite close.

I waited for a few minutes after pressing send. He had been waiting online and a six line reply eventually filtered into my inbox. I began to get excited as he said he was from Penrith, and confirmed his fantasy again and said he would cover all expenses for me to travel to him. It was important, he said, that the game was played out in his home town where a handful of people he knew would see us together.

Where the hell was Penrith? Wasn't that in Scotland somewhere?

Penrith wasn't in Scotland but it was a fair journey, up near the Lake District in Cumbria. We exchanged a few emails and he gave me directions, said I could travel first class by train and that he would meet me at the station.

The man, who I'll call Neil, was nice, around fifty years old and was a QC. He wanted me to act like his spoilt sugar baby whilst shopping for a few things and then once we settled in a bar it was my job to get the drinks down him, tricking him into getting tipsy enough so that he wouldn't argue with my request to hand over his money. It seemed simple enough. We discussed what I would wear, a tight fitting pink cashmere jumper, skin tight light coloured jeans and a pair of Louboutin stilettos. My hair was to be in curls or waves and I was expected to be heavily made up and insisted on pink glossy lips.

"'I want men to stare at you," his final mail said. "I want them to want to be me."

I could understand the ego boost but this type of scenario puzzled me, he wasn't a submissive as such but he liked the thought of being taken advantage of whilst shopping and then wanted his wallet raped? It all sounded too good to be true, as it had with the loser and yet I knew these men existed. When my first class ticket arrived in the post I had no hesitation preparing for the trip

I knew I would have to be a little flirtatious as well as bratty so I kept that in mind as I applied my make up in the train toilets twenty minutes before Penrith, I smiled, I was actually enjoying the work and realised I had no hang ups or nervousness whatsoever.

I stepped from the train suited and booted and ready to act like a bratty conniving bitch for the rest of the day.

He was dressed as he said he would be in a pair of designer jeans, white shirt and expensive looking black jacket with Oakley sun-glasses perched on his semi balding forehead as I approached the news store we were meeting at.

"Hello darling," he smiled confidently, leaning over to kiss my cheek.

"Hi honey," I responded loudly in the girliest voice I could muster. My God, passers-by were already looking at us but it was exactly what he craved. I tried not to blush. I sidled up to him a little closer as I stroked at his sleeve.

"I can't wait to go shopping; you did promise me a few nice things."

"Yes, yes," he mumbled looking around at the other passengers and revelling in the attention, "but be careful" he said, "my cards have limits and we don't want to go upsetting my bank managers do we?"

I nodded my agreement and we were off, striding purposely in the direction of the first shop.

He threw me a little in the shops as he took control of the shopping list. This was not like the session with the loser where I had a free reign to choose what I liked and although I was a little put out at first I recalled the content of his e-mails, which focused in on the wallet rape. I reminded myself to be patient as he filled two carrier bags of slutty underwear, then bought me a short tight dress. As we walked from the department store I teased him a little and begged him to buy me a selection of cosmetics of my choice, which he did. I linked his arm and thanked him several times as he punched his credit card details into the machine telling the shop assistant that I was a liability but worth every penny. She looked at me with daggers as I gave him a little peck on the cheek.

"It was time," he announced. Now the fun would start.

We headed to a cocktail and champagne bar and settled at the table near the window. "I'm going to the gents," he said. "Can you remember what to do?"

I nodded. As he walked away I called the waiter over and ordered a bottle of Bollinger. As soon as he was out of sight I whispered into the waiter's ear.

"Excuse me," I said, "my boyfriend here wants us to get drunk but to be quite honest I'm not really in the mood. If possible whenever I order shots of vodka, can you make sure the shot you give to me is just water please?"

The waiter looked at me as if I was on drugs.

"You want me to bring water instead of vodka?" he said with a frown on his face.

"Yes," I said, "obviously without his knowledge and of course charge vodka prices for the water and put the difference straight in your pocket."

I smiled and slid a twenty pound note across the table.

"It will be our secret of course."

The waiter's eyes lit up.

"No problem Miss," he winked.

My QC friend was still quite bossy and loud. He was nice but loved to show his authority, this was about to change as the ice bucket of Bollinger arrived.

The waiter was right on cue. "Would you like anything else Sir.. Miss?"

"Yes." I said taking control. "Two vodkas straight up, a little ice and lemon and two tequilas please."

As the drink flowed I could see a shift in his mood as I flirted a little and teased him about our afternoon shopping. I told him there were lots of other things I could buy which would make our evenings together a whole lot better. I handed him another fresh glass of tequila.

"Drink up honey," I cooed as I hung my arms around his neck planting gentle kisses on his cheeks.

He reached for the glass blushing.

"You're not going to take advantage of me darling?" he said, "Just because I've had one too many."

I leaned into him even further, lifting the glass to his lips forcing him to take a mouthful.

"You're going to be a good boy and do whatever I say aren't you?" I smirked changing my tone to a more dominant manner; I could hear him groan. Now I was getting somewhere.

"Drink up," I ordered. "There's a good boy."

He downed the tequila in one and I became aware of the perspiration standing out on his brow. I stood up and peered over onto his lap.

His erect penis resembled a tent poll as it strained against the material of his high quality jeans.

"Oh my, someone is enjoying themselves, is it because you know I'm going to rinse you?"

He was lost for words, reaching for another glass that wasn't there. I beckoned the waiter over and ordered another vodka and a tequila. I thought the waiter was about to blow my story as he gave me the strangest of looks but he nodded politely and walked back to the bar smiling.

I leaned over and stroked the inside of his thigh with my foot. For a second I was almost getting turned on myself realising that it had been some months since I'd been laid. I made a mental note that I had to do something to remedy that, only not with Neil. He was nice but not that nice, this was just business.

"Give me your wallet dear." I said. I held out my hand laughing at him as he shifted in his seat. "You want to keep me happy don't you my darling?"

"Oh yes, yes of course," he panted, reaching into his pocket, taking it out slowly. He held it in mid-air for a tantalising second or two.

"Give it here now," I demanded and before he could object I moved swiftly forward and snatched it out of his hand. I eased back into my seat leering at him as I slowly opened the wallet. I counted it in front of him as I lifted four crisp fifties and six tens and slipped them into my handbag. I had to compose myself and remember that this was what this sad specimen wanted.

If the session had ended right there and then I would have been a happy girl, well remunerated for the service I had provided but his email had said there would be a lot more than this on offer and I sensed that this was just the beginning.

I sighed, shaking my head.

"This simply won't do will it?" I leant back in my chair waiting for his reply.

"Uh no, I guess not," he mumbled.

The waiter arrived with the drinks and before he'd left the table I had forced the tequila in front of him.

"Drink," I demanded as I sipped at my glass of fake vodka. I took a debit card from his wallet and drew it seductively across my neck, caressing my skin and moving it down towards my cleavage.

"You do want me to be happy," I said, "because when I'm happy I like to make you happy my darling."

He was nodding now, incapable of words and the saliva was forming in the corner of his mouth.

"Come," I said, "we're going to the damn cashpoint and you're going to make me happy." I stood as I pulled on my jacket and noticed he was breathing hard. I signalled for the cheque and told him to pay it.

I waited outside tapping my foot impatiently – for effect of course – he stumbled out the door, well on the way to being half pissed. Part of me felt this was wrong and yet I was aware that this was exactly what he wanted. His erection was almost bursting through his zip, this was really turning him on, there was no doubt about it.

"This way," I said as I looked up and down the street spotting the familiar blue sign of the Barclays Bank Eagle. Good old Barclays, a cashpoint on every high street in the country. I was about to take my client to the cleaners, take advantage of him at his request and remembered I had seen three bank cards in his wallet. He'd told me in the email that his cards had a maximum withdrawal allowance of two hundred and fifty pounds per day. Was it realistic that he would let me relieve him of seven hundred and fifty pounds?

There was only one way to find out as I strode purposely towards the Barclays hole in the wall. I reached the machine and leant against the wall smirking as he came towards me. He was swaying and bumping into the wall a few times with a ridiculous look of satisfaction on his face. I looked down; his bulging cock was clearly visible in his trousers, he was enjoying every second.

"You are a naughty boy," I laughed staring at his jeans.

I took the lapel of his jacket and gave it a little tug.

"What's the pin number of this card?" I said holding it in front of his face.

"And no pissing around."

I fluttered my eyelashes and spoke ever so softly.

"You do want me to be happy don't you?"

"Yes I do, I really do," he said.

I stroked a finger across his cheekbone.

"Good boy. So what's the pin?" I asked as I slipped the first card into the slot of the machine.

He appeared to hesitate for a second and for a moment I thought it was all going to come crashing down. I remembered somebody once saying that if something seemed too good to be true than it probably was. I still had his lapel and I pulled him nearer to the machine with my fingers poised over the buttons. I had forgotten my act temporarily and that's what had caused him to stall. My other hand wandered down to his groin area as I brushed the back of my knuckles across the top of his belt.

"The pin number. Now!" I demanded. "Or I'm getting straight back on the train and you'll never see me again."

"six seven four five, it's six seven four five," he cried out desperately as my hand lingered on his belt.

I smiled, gave him a peck on the cheek and then turned and tapped in the numbers. The machine gave a little whirring noise and there were a few seconds of silence before the slot opened up under the screen and five fifty pound notes slid into site. I reached down and took them as I held them up in front of his face.

"There you are," I said, "that wasn't too difficult now, was it?"

"No darling," he replied.

I took out the next card,

"Pin number," I said. "What's the pin?"

Again he appeared to pause. This was his game, his act and by now I knew exactly what was expected of me.

"Look, you sad fucking specimen, stop dicking me about. We can do this my way or no way at all," I said. "You're aching for me and you can have me but only if you give me what I want first."

"Yes darling," he said.

"And if I don't get what I want then I'll walk away and leave you here with your precious fucking cards and your lonely hard on, do you hear?"

"six seven four five," he said. "They're all the same pin number, six seven four five."

I couldn't believe my luck as I withdrew two hundred and fifty pounds on a second bank card and another two hundred and fifty pounds on the third. I couldn't get my head around it as I stuffed the cash into my purse and I was just about to hand his wallet over when I noticed two more cards in another section. I grinned as I teased them out of his wallet, a Visa and a Mastercard.

"Oh look," I said. "See what we have here, I nearly missed them."

"No please," he said, "I'll be charged for cash withdrawals, you can't use them."

It was time for some real drama. I scowled at him as I threw his wallet into his chest, turned on my heels and I stormed away. Within three or four steps he had caught up begging me to take them.

"Take them, take them," he pleaded. "They are for you, please take them, I'm sorry. Please stay a little longer."

He led me back to the machine like a man possessed as he took out the maximum cash allowance on each credit card.

"Take it all," he said, shoving bundles of cash into my bag and then he begged me for one more drink in a hotel bar.

The job was nearing its conclusion. The email explained that the role play finished with him booking a hotel room and in full view of everybody in the reception area we were to wobble up to the room together and everybody would think he was going to fuck my brains out all evening.

The George Hotel was situated in Penrith on the main street. It was quite small and had a nice family atmosphere and was very busy. It was exactly what Neil the QC had in mind as he convinced the receptionist through the alcohol fumes that we needed a room for at least one night, possibly two. I smiled at the other patrons as they looked on in disbelief at the balding middle-aged man and his tart of a girlfriend. I pinched his bum and smothered him with seductive kisses and shows of affection as he paid for the room on the Visa credit card I had just maxed out at the cashpoint. We then retired to the bar area where he took yet another tequila and I had a genuine glass of champagne this time. After about forty minutes I stood up and noisily demanded that he take me to the room. As we walked across the bar area I physically prevented him from crashing into a full table of drinks but eventually managed to get him into the lift which took us to the third floor. Room three zero three was ten metres along the passage and I inserted the key, opened the door and bundled him through onto the bed.

He started to get all lecherous in the privacy of the room and had conveniently forgotten the terms and conditions of the contract. I stood over him as he tried to pull his trousers off and barter with me for some additional services. I refused and within three or four minutes he was sleeping like a baby. I took a shower in the room, removed my tarts make-up and toned down my hair as I blow-dried it. Neil was snoring like a stuffed pig as I left the room and walked along the corridor. I buttoned my coat up just before I walked through reception and convinced myself that the girl behind the desk didn't recognise the slapper who had breezed in like a bull in a china shop earlier that afternoon.

I couldn't wait to get back on the train and made a point of booking myself an evening dinner in the restaurant car. Don't let anyone tell you British rail food is crap because it's not. I had a pleasant prawn and avocado starter followed by a lemon chicken dish and washed it all down with the obligatory champagne. There is something exquisite about eating good food and drinking expensive champagne while watching the English countryside pass by. It was an incredibly satisfying experience particularly when you have over two thousand pounds stuffed in your handbag.

I couldn't believe it. I wanted to squeal and thump the table and shout out loud, what a bloody great day I'd just had.

Some weeks later I had an almost identical session with Neil only this time without the role play of the hotel. He left me and I walked away and stopped at a coffee shop on the way to the station. On sheer impulse I rang him. To this day I don't know what made me do it.

"Have you had a nice day Neil?"

"Yes Mistress."

"Don't think I'm finished with you yet," I said. "Get your lazy arse to the cashpoint and get me another hundred pounds. I'm out with the girls tonight and I'm going to need a little extra."

Without hesitation that's exactly what he did as he walked sheepishly into the coffee shop and placed it on the table. I ignored him, picked the cash up and placed it in my handbag.

"Will that be all Mistress?" he asked.

With a flick of my hand I waved him off and he scurried away like a little mouse.

He sent me an email when he arrived home; he said that was the best bit about the entire day because it had been my impulse and my decision to take the game that one step further.

Oh my gosh, is that not bizarre?

Chapter Eight

It was a great feeling knowing that I was no longer obligated to the club, and although I had been a little anxious about where my money would come from I now felt like a weight had been lifted from my shoulders. The girls were sad to see me leave and had organised a night out in the city and I was really looking forward to it. I took out my iPhone and blocked out Wednesday afternoon and promised myself a shopping trip to buy the perfect outfit for the occasion. I dropped an email to the beauty salon and asked them if they could give me a facial first thing on Friday morning. Their email box was well attended to, and within three minutes they had replied that they could fit me in at ten that morning I typed back 'perfect.' I was feeling like a million dollars.

I opened another email, a new client wanting a real time session for one hour in the privacy of his own home. This was a little nerve-wracking because I'd always felt uncomfortable about going to clients' houses and yet he was offering five hundred pounds for a one hour session. I wanted to say no and yet I was feeling indestructible. I wondered what he wanted. My fingers hovered over the reply button. It wouldn't do any harm to ask. I could always say no. So I asked him what he wanted and nearly choked on my food when I read his reply.

'I will be naked sat in front of a table full of custard pies. There will be about two hundred of them. I want you to throw them at me until I come.'

What the fuck?
I typed back.

'I think you're taking the mickey my dear.'

'I'm not. If you can't fulfil my fantasy I'll understand.'

He wasn't pushy. Could he be for real? I messaged him again and said I was uncomfortable about going to his home address. Again he said he understood but I had to understand why it couldn't be carried out in a hotel room. He gave me his address and told me to drive by and meet him beforehand if that made me feel easier. I didn't answer him immediately, instead I Googled his address and found it on street view. It was very upmarket, this guy whoever he was had money. I decided to push him a little further and said I would do it for seven hundred as it was out of my normal territory and meant quite a bit of travelling.

He agreed and said he would credit my account there and then.

He did. The money was there within thirty minutes and he emailed me back giving me four different times and days and further instructions.

Holy crap! I couldn't back out now. So I picked a time and said I would be happy to do business with him.

Going about my daily errands I found myself studying some of the men I sat next to on the subway or passed me by on the street, each time wandering if they had any dark desires or strange fetishes and realised that my thoughts were drifting to sex once again. This was happening more and more recently, probably because although my clients weren't turning me on by any stretch of the imagination, the subject of sex was well and truly on the menu and it was getting to me.

The next day was the real time session with the custard pies and as I neared his house I was having second thoughts. It was fifteen minutes before our appointment as I pulled alongside the entrance of the estate. This was serious money country, with BMWs, Mercs and Porsches littering the street. Four wheeled drives and top of the range people carriers were parked on the block paved entranceways and there was hardly a leaf or a blade of grass out of place. Surely a psychopath couldn't be hiding behind one of these doors? I checked my handbag for my Mace and pulled it into the top compartment, just in case. At five minutes to eleven I drove the car up to the door and got out and walked warily up the driveway. He looked nice (they all do), dressed in a thick navy blue bathrobe. He asked me in, shaking my hand gently and as I took a deep breath I walked through the door. This is absolutely the worst moment seeing a new client for a real time session. I suppose it's the danger factor that once inside they could attack you and do anything they wanted to do. I didn't know this man from Adam and yet he was obviously successful, very rich and looked nothing like a mass murderer. I also made sure I had walked up the drive when a neighbour had walked by with her dog figuring that if she had seen me and the client had noticed her too then he would be reluctant to try any funny business.

But from the outset I felt at ease. He made me a coffee and reaffirmed exactly what it was he wanted from me.

"I'm all ready for you," he said. "The custard pies are stacked up in the other reception room."

He laughed. "They're not real custard of course. I find shaving foam works far better."

I couldn't hold back any longer. "Look Bob, (name changed) I'm a little uncomfortable with this I mean it's..."

"Not normal," he interjected, "and what is normal? Are threesomes normal and homosexuality and fucking your wife up the arse and making her dress up as French maid? Is that normal? And what about the paedophiles and the flashers, the men who want to be pissed and shit on because that's the only way they can get a hard on? Who is it that defines normality at the end of the day?"

Wow! Bob's little tirade took me by surprise and I suppose he did have a point. Before I could answer he continued.

"I can't help the way I feel but even you must admit when it comes to sexual fetishes this one is rather harmless and it hurts no one and I'm the one who has to clean up the mess."

I was thinking about the sandwich man, surely Bob was right, at least this wouldn't turn my stomach like that dirty bastard had.

So we talked a little more, but not too much because I make a point of never asking my clients why a certain situation turns them on. I'll admit I'm curious to know sometimes but unless they blurt it out it's best to be left in the dark because quite frankly I don't think I could handle it.

"I love the feel of the foam on my naked body."

Bob brought me back from my thoughts.

"And I love the noise the pies make when they hit me."

He looked me in the eye as I sat like a frozen zombie. "And of course I want you to abuse me and swear at me too."

I nodded in agreement, I was happy at that last statement... I was in familiar territory.

"If you don't mind we'll get started now."

Strangely enough I was now completely at ease and Bob stood and led me into the room where it would all happen. There were at least a dozen empty shaving foam canisters on the floor and a table loaded up with paper plates covered in perfectly prepared custard pies. On the far side of the room the wall was covered top to bottom in clear polythene sheeting as was the carpet two metres out. As per his instructions I stripped down to my black bra and panties and Bob dispensed with the bath robe leaving him as naked as the day he was born. I stepped into my role.

"Get the fuck over there you hopeless piece of shit."

Bob walked over onto the polythene took up his position and cowered in the corner as I threw the first few custard pies. It was a little difficult at first and I cursed as the first ones sailed harmlessly by and splattered onto the wall behind him. But he was patient and I eventually I got the hang of it and my aim became better. Within a few minutes he was covered from head to foot in shaving foam, begging me for more and I'll admit I was having the time of my life. This was bloody great fun. After ten minutes I was sweating freely and glad that I was nearly naked as I gauged I was only half way through the pies. As I got down to the last fifty Bob started jacking off and I screamed out more and more abuse until about ten pies before the end he ejaculated, slipped on the foam and collapsed in a heap. I couldn't believe the end result. Picture the scene, a butt naked, grown man lying in several inches of shaving foam mixed with a little spunk panting hard but with a smile on his face wider than the Mersey Tunnel. He hadn't disgusted me like the sandwich man and of course I never stopped thinking about my hourly rate, which always helps. I also wondered if I was becoming used to these weird people and somehow becoming hardened to the nature of the job, desensitised I think they call it.

Bob cleaned himself up and I wiped myself down and got dressed. He offered me another coffee or 'something stronger' but I politely declined. I quite liked Bob, but didn't want to go overboard. This was business I reminded myself and the last thing I wanted was to get friendly with my clients.

But Bob asked if I could come again and I didn't hesitate and said I would. Another few Bobs would do nicely thank you very much.

Saturday night couldn't come quick enough. As I got ready I sipped champagne a slave had given me as a gift and looked at my outfit laid out on the bed bought for me by a willing submissive. He had bought a short black, Jersey silk backless dress and a pair of silver Jimmy Choo stilettos. I grinned a broad grin of satisfaction as I stared down on them. My life was taking a rather strange direction, but one that I was more than comfortable with. The only thing that bothered me was that I didn't really have anyone to talk to about it. I wasn't ashamed of what I was doing because I was fulfilling a service and more than that, satisfying a select, if not strange group of individuals. But of course this wasn't normal and some would see me as two steps away from a prostitute which I wasn't. But I think the main reason I didn't want to talk to anyone about it was because this was something different and very easy money and part of me wondered how many clients were out there. One thing was for sure, if I blabbed about it too much, some of my friends might want to get in on the act, after all it was a lot easier than dancing and the wages were higher too.

I arrived at the first bar where we were all meeting, excited at the prospect of the night ahead. The girls were all impeccably dressed and caused a little stir and lots of stares from the opposite sex.

After a few drinks we went on to a club where we had a VIP table waiting for us, courtesy of the manager who frequented the club most of the girls worked in. As we walked through the already busy club I did a quick scan of the men. Nothing took my fancy; perhaps I still wasn't ready for sex as I couldn't see anyone I was remotely interested in. Was it wrong that I seemed to be almost obsessed at how a man looked? I was fussy, I'll admit that, my man had to be attractive and fit looking and he had to dress well before he caught my eye and at times I almost regretted setting my goals so high. But I couldn't help it, Mother Nature at work.

I pushed these thoughts to the back of my head as they always drifted back to David. He was after all responsible for my sexual drought and the sole reason I now disliked the vast majority of men so much.

As we arrived at the VIP area we were seated at a large table and served drinks. There was just one table opposite us, still empty with a large gold reserved sign next to a champagne bucket. Other than that it was quite busy and the atmosphere was good.

After another couple of bottles of champagne a group of guys (we were told they were former Etonians) came over and started eyeing up the girls. They asked if they could join us and we agreed if they could afford the entrance fee of two bottles of Cristal. They were quite good looking and very friendly and one of them took charge as he called a waiter over and slid his gold card onto the tray. Within minutes the two bottles were at our table and the Eton boys sat down.

I like to people watch so as the others were larking around I sat there totally mesmerised by the toffs who were indulging in champagne and a little 'Charles,' popping off to the toilet more frequently than necessary. It was clear what they were up to but obviously loaded with money so the management and the bouncers turned a convenient blind eye. Their confidence grew after each visit; it was almost comical as they came on to my friends' big style. The girls seemed to enjoy the attention as the four well-spoken men cracked jokes and served up a heap of compliments. It probably happened by accident but as there were six of us, two girls were going to be left out on a limb. That was me and my friend Summer but we just sat back, quite happy and relaxed as we watched the mating game develop.

It was midnight when I first noticed him, he was positively beautiful and I tried to keep my jaw from smashing to the floor as he and another gentleman walked up to the red VIP rope and were shown to the reserved table opposite us. He caught my gaze and stared straight at me as I squirmed uncomfortably in my large velvet chair. I was aware of the effect he had on me and the return of the feelings I had not experienced for a long time. He was gorgeous – without a doubt.

"Oh my God," whispered Summer, "have you seen him?"

"I can't take my eyes off him," I said.

I was glad of the low level lighting as I could feel myself turning bright red. I broke the stare and turned to Summer.

"Holy shit, he's absolutely gorgeous."

Summer was looking over my shoulder, casually stealing an occasional glance.

"He's amazing and totally into you," Summer said, "he can't take his eyes off you."

And I could feel it too; I could feel his eyes burning into my back.

"Jess, he hasn't stopped watching you since he walked in, oh my God he is perfect," she cooed.

I turned around and pretended to look for a waiter and we made eye contact again. He was the most gorgeous man I had ever seen, he was very well dressed, looked like he had the body of what I can only describe as an Adonis, a chiselled face with piercing dark eyes and jet black hair immaculately styled. He looked like a businessman and so very sure of himself but not in an arrogant way, he was sexy and had a presence. I assumed he was around mid-thirties and stood around six foot or a little taller. I turned back towards Summer, desperately trying to compose myself.

"Mmm, you know his mate is not bad either," she said, craning her neck over me to check out his friend.

She stood and waved.

"Hello," she called over.

"Oh my God," I said, "what the hell are you doing, don't please, oh my God let the ground open up," I ranted, but she was already on her way over.

I turned around and there he was staring again, no expression, coolness personified.

I looked at Summer as she sat down next to his friend who was also very handsome but not in the way 'he' was. He leaned forward and pulled a large velvet chair out from the table, beckoning me to join him. I was trembling like a leaf in a hurricane but I slowly reached for my clutch bag, stood and walked over. I tried to stay cool, refusing to make eye contact with this man who had this ridiculous effect on me as Summer introduced us.

As I sat down he pulled his hand away brushing the base of my back, my whole body seemed to tingle. His hand felt large and powerful, it made my body jolt and I quickly stood up. I didn't know why I had stood up and was aware that I now looked stupid. I felt as if the whole club was staring at me.

"Um, excuse me I'm just going to the ladies," I muttered, leaving the table in double quick time.

Summer was so engrossed in her catch she didn't even notice I'd gone. I scurried off to the toilets to try and sort myself out.

The VIP restroom had a large washroom, very over the top decor with marble and gold and two large velvet chaise longue chairs and on each side of the rest room there were two more doors leading to the female and male cubicles. The whole area was empty as I walked in and closed the door behind me. I stood staring into the mirror and wanted to give myself a slap. Shit, what was wrong with me, this guy hadn't even spoken to me and it was already eating me alive, come on sort yourself out and stop acting so timid and plain weird. I looked at my reflection and opened my clutch, touching up my makeup in an attempt to calm myself down. Don't blow it I thought, he's perfect and if Summer is right, that he can't take his eyes off me, then I'm in with a chance. It sounds bizarre but he was the only man I'd met since the breakup with David I could imagine being with. I closed up my bag and checked my reflection one more time, the dress was gorgeous, it clung to all the right places and the back was just high enough that it grazed the top of my bum. I looked at where his hand had touched me. I trembled again; my God I wanted him so badly. I walked through the loo door, realising when I got in there that I didn't need to go to the toilet, turned round and made my way back into the unisex washroom. As I opened the door and walked out a strong hand grabbed my wrist and almost threw me back through into the cubicle area.

It was him. He had pushed me up against the wall, one hand held me hard by the shoulder; his other held my jaw as he stared down at me. He didn't smile but his eyes danced like a cat playing with a mouse. He pushed his lips against mine moving his hand from my jawline towards the nape of my neck as he kissed me hard. I felt absolutely helpless as he reached around my head and grabbed a handful of my hair and pulled my head back slipping his tongue into my mouth as he pushed against me pressing me hard against the wall. I couldn't even think. I was totally taken by surprise and it was turning me on like I could never have imagined. Eventually I responded, my hands moved up his hard, muscular body until they were finally around his neck and in his hair. The kisses were more rushed and urgent as his tongue searched mine and our breathing synchronised as one. He slid his other hand gently down my bare back and inside my dress tracing the outline of my G-string and the feeling was electric as an exquisite shiver ran the length of my spine. My God I was on the point of orgasm, what was happening to me? He reached for my arms around his neck and grasped them hard pushing them above my head and pinned them above me to the wall. I felt helpless, I had no control but I loved every second, it felt amazing. I didn't even know him and yet I felt in no danger, the only feelings that were coursing through me were that of sheer ecstasy and animalistic passion. His hand moved up and down my back and the kissing now grew slower but harder and deeper and I could feel his hard cock pressing against my stomach and I wanted him like I have never wanted a man before. Suddenly he stopped and pulled away. He looked at me with a scowl etched across his face.

"You are a naughty girl making me do this," he whispered as he continued to run his hand up and down my back. "Do you often hangout in restrooms waiting for strange men to seduce you?"

He grinned, a cheeky, confident grin.

"Come," he ordered. "We're leaving right now."

He bent down to pick up my bag that had been thrown into the corner. I still couldn't believe what the hell had just happened but I didn't want it to stop either.

"Give me a minute please," I gasped, aware that I was struggling for breath.

"Certainly Jessica," he smiled again.

I smiled at him.

"You know my name, I don't know yours."

"Edward," he said and with that he left closing the door behind him.

I quickly checked my appearance, I looked flustered and even though we hadn't gone very far, I had that 'just fucked glow,' hanging over me. I ran a brush through my hair and reapplied some gloss to my tender, swollen but satisfied lips.

He was waiting for me as I walked out and held out his hand by way of an invitation. I smiled and slipped my hand into his as he led me back to the table.

He spoke to his friend. "Jessica and I have had enough of this place, we are going. Do you want me to send Andrew back for you?" he asked.

"Who's Andrew?" I asked.

"My driver," he said casually. "He's waiting outside."

His friend placed a hand on Summer's knee.

"No, we will get a taxi," he replied as he fixed his eyes on Summer and she smiled and blushed like a love struck teenager.

Jesus, I thought. How has this happened so quickly? One minute Summer and I were quite content with a little people watching and a drink or two and now here we were both contemplating spending the night with two men we'd only known for half an hour at the most.

His driver was waiting out the back of the club in a private bay. A black Range Rover, with tinted, blackened windows. It was like something from a Men In Black movie.

This was strange, who was this guy? I was a little put off by the fact this man had a driver; it was a little too much.

"Who are you Edward?" I asked. "What do you do, work for MI5 or something?"

He smiled.

"Nothing quite as exciting as that I'm afraid. I have a few businesses and most of them do quite well. I work hard Jessica and having a driver is one of the things I promised myself since I was young. Andrew is more like a good friend and we go back a long way. He drives me and guides me throughout my working day and when I fancy an odd night out he's there for me too."

It was all a little unreal as Andrew doffed his cap in my direction, opened the door and helped me in. Edward climbed in and sat close to me as he wrapped his arm around my shoulders. As the car glided away he placed his free hand on my knee, toying with the inside of my thigh for what seemed like a long journey. My heart skipped beat after beat as he ran his hand up and down my leg until we reached the destination. We were still in the city, outside a tall block of what looked like expensive apartments. A uniformed man stood just inside the door and I waited in the lobby making polite conversation with him as Edward spoke to Andrew for a few minutes.

I was a little unsure as to whether I wanted to take things further and the first signs of nerves kicked in. I didn't know this man and I was not a lover of one night stands! Not many women are, some in fact swear they would never do such a thing, but there is always that one person that drives them crazy enough to want to do it.

My thoughts were interrupted as he walked towards me; he slipped his arm around my waist and directed me towards the elevator. I could feel him staring at me again but I chose to fight the urge to look up at him and instead watched the numbers flash by as the elevator hurtled skywards. The doors opened and he took a firm hold of my hand as he led me towards the door of his apartment. The alcohol was now wearing off and I was a little nervous at the prospect of having sex with this perfect man because that was what the inevitable conclusion would be if I walked through that door.

He took out a key and inserted it into the lock, pushed the door open and led me inside.

He hit a switch lighting up the large apartment. It was stunning, a beautiful plush, off white carpet with minimum but expensive looking furnishings. He reached for the switch again and the lights in the apartment dimmed and I focused on the lights of the city twinkling several stories below us.

"Wow, what an amazing view," I murmured.

"Champagne?"

I nodded.

I heard the pop of the cork as he opened the champagne and he walked over to me handing me a glass.

We sat down on the luxurious oversized black and white leather sofa positioned to take in the best view of the city below. He was sitting with his feet up on the sofa with his back up against the armrest. He leaned over and turned me so that my back was towards him. I heard him placing his glass on the large marble coffee table then I felt his hands in my hair. I almost dropped my glass as my heart started to race. He gathered my long hair and gently placed it over my shoulder as he pushed me gently forward and traced his fingers down my spine. My God, the sensation was electrifying; I could feel my body jumping and the goose bumps forming over my entire body as I became acutely aware of my nipples hardening. His large hands started to knead my shoulders, I could feel his warm breath on my neck. I felt his lips on the back of my neck as he began kissing me ever so slowly and I began to melt, my whole body giving in to his touch. Without warning he slipped my dress forward and pushed it down around my waist exposing my nakedness and my champagne glass fell onto the carpet. His kisses worked all over my neck up to my jaw line. He spun me back to face him as he pulled me onto his lap. I was straddling him and could feel his erection bursting through his trousers as I kissed him. He purred as I ran my fingers through his hair then he pushed my hair over my shoulders exposing my breasts. He stopped kissing me for a moment as he studied my naked form. He grinned as he slid a hand around my waist, pushed me away from him and bent his head down to take one of my nipples in his mouth.

I couldn't control myself at this point as I tried to undo the buttons of his crisp white shirt but the more he flicked his tongue over my nipple the more desperate I was becoming. My patience snapped as I took two handfuls of shirt and ripped it apart. Little buttons flew everywhere.

"Naughty little girl Jessica," he mumbled as he removed his mouth from my breast. "Very naughty."

He grabbed my dress bunched around my waist and pulled it over my head throwing it onto the floor. He kissed me hard as his fingers traced my panties and I ground back and forth over his erection. He stood up as I wrapped my legs tightly around his waist. He walked me towards the window still kissing me frantically and I felt the cold glass on my back. My first thoughts were that someone could see in but deep within the throes of passion I just didn't care.

"Hold on," he whispered as he undid his trousers.

I clung tighter, kissing him harder and biting his lip, waiting for what was about to be the night of my life. I heard the trousers and his belt hit the floor and he grabbed roughly at my underwear and ripped it from my body. He pushed me back against the glass as I wrapped myself around his torso and he entered me.

"Holy shit," I gasped. "Oh my God, oh my fucking God."

The sensation of being sandwiched between the cold glass and his hot damp body was spine tingling, unreal, as he thrust into me kissing me even harder working his tongue between my teeth. His thrusts were harder and faster as I felt a fire racing through my body.

"I'm going to come, oh my God, oh my God."

This was like nothing I'd ever experienced before, Christ what was happening to me?

Edward sensed I was on the verge of a climax and picked up the pace as he slammed me against the window again and again.

I was on the point of no return now as I exploded and dug my nails deep into his back as I came. My orgasm lingered for what seemed like an age and a split second later Edward tensed up and cried out loudly as I felt him swell up inside me. He trembled ever so gently as he came, his lips centimetres from mine as I hung loosely around his neck. As our breathing slowed and we held onto each other tightly I eventually lowered my aching legs to the floor and we held each other for several seconds as our breathing returned to normal

My head was spinning; he kissed me again and smiled. He swung an arm underneath me and lifted me into his arms and carried me to a giant marble bathroom. He opened the door to a huge step-in shower cubicle and turned the tap as the room filled with steam. He lowered me to the floor, stepped in and beckoned me to join him holding out his hand, which I took without hesitation.

"You will stay a while won't you Jess?" he asked.

"Yes," I said. "I'll stay for as long as you want me too."

Chapter Nine

I awoke the next morning with sunlight streaming through the large windows picking out the particles of dust floating in the air. At first I didn't realise where I was as the surroundings were alien to me. But gradually it came to me. Did that really happen I thought, did we really do that, did I really just spend the night with this amazing looking man?

I looked over and Edward was still sleeping. I took a moment to just take him in and couldn't help myself as an involuntary smile pulled across my face. His face was beautiful, everything I had remembered from the night before and yet in the cold light of day it was as if it was even more real than the night before. It wasn't a dream, my perfect man was lying here right beside me. I leaned on my elbow and watched him sleeping for several minutes almost willing him to wake and catch me watching him to see what his reaction would be. Surely he must do some sort of male modelling, he clearly loved the gym. The sheet was bunched around his waist and I bit my lip as I studied his abs as they lifted gently up and down in time with his breathing.

I slowly lifted myself from under the sheets, retrieved my clutch bag and crept towards the en-suite, another overdone bathroom, large with lots and lots of marble, very clean and yet with a masculine touch if that's possible.

I couldn't believe the sex I had just had a few hours ago as I slipped into the shower and stood under the water for some time. I wanted the noise to wake him, I wanted him to slip in here beside me and take me again. It wasn't to be. I took a quick look in the bedroom as I stepped from the shower and he was still sleeping like a baby. Not to worry. I searched for a spare tooth brush and emptied the contents of my bag, brushed my hair and washed my face applying a little bronzer, mascara and lip gloss.

I instinctively reached for my phone. There was a missed call and a message from Mum, 'Morning dear, hope you had good night? What time shall I drop Russell back?' and a message from Summer which read simply, 'Oh my gosh.' I laughed out loud wondering what sort of night she'd had. Surely it couldn't have been as special as mine?

I tiptoed back into the room. Still sleeping. What should I do? I was still naked so I bit my lip and went for it slipping under the covers not so gently this time, determined to wake him. I needed to know how he would react. The suspense was killing me.

He stirred, his eyes fluttered open and he smiled, yes he definitely smiled.

"Well hello Jess... good morning."

I grinned, trying not to feel embarrassed now that I was stone cold sober. What would he do? Make mad passionate love to me like he had last night?

"Can I make us some coffee," he asked studying me carefully.

"Sure, coffee would be great," I mumbled trying to mask my disappointment and confusion.

He gave me a quick kiss on the cheek and slipped out of bed. Holy shit the body, it was amazing from behind too. I tried not to stare as he walked away butt naked, grabbed two white robes from the closet, turned around and came back towards me placing one at the foot of the huge bed and slipping the other over his perfect body.

"I'll be in the kitchen," he called out leaving the room.

Oh no! I'd blown it and I knew it. This was exactly why you shouldn't do one night stands. And why had he asked me to stay and then climbed out of bed? I felt a horrible ache in the pit of my stomach. I really liked him and yet he didn't try anything this morning instead he was busy making coffee and wasn't giving anything away.

"Arghhh," I groaned out loud smashing my fists into the duck down quilt that engulfed me.

"For Christ sake," I muttered as I sat up and got out of the bed. I put on the robe and took a quick look in the mirror. Oh yes very sexy, not! I'm not surprised, I was exhausted, I'd hardly slept a wink all night and even the sneaky shower and make up touch up didn't help in hiding that fact.

Frowning and feeling cheap I walked out of the bedroom into the huge open plan living area concentrating hard trying to look cool and unfazed. It was so bright in there as the morning sun bounced of the excessive white walls and sparsely furnished room, making me feel exposed and vulnerable with nowhere to hide. I wanted a dimmer switch to control the light but it was not to be. I pulled the robe tight around me and stared out of the windows looking at the city below. Eventually I plucked up the courage, turned away from *that* window and walked towards the breakfast bar where he stood waiting for the coffee machine to do its thing.

"Milk?" he said.

"Please," I replied coolly.

He handed me a cup and gestured for me to follow him to the sofa. I grimaced as I pictured the urgent, hard sex we had had right here a few hours ago. Now I felt so embarrassed and willed him to put me at ease with a few well-chosen words. But before he could say anything I caught sight of the piano in the far corner. How hadn't I seen that last night?

"Do you play?" I asked, desperately trying to make small talk. "Or is it just for show?"

He laughed. "Yes I do play as it happens, not very well but I can bash out a few tunes."

I was just about to beg him to play when he stood and walked over to the gleaming black piano and sat down. He lifted the piano lid and flexed his fingers and flicked through a music book above the keyboard. I studied him for a moment as he studied the book and then he leaned into the piano and started to play.

He was brilliant – of course he was. The music filled the whole room and sent a shiver running the length of my spine. It was so good, what a talent, effortless. It lasted no more than three minutes and as he closed the lid again he smiled and announced that was all I was getting.

"You really are very good."

I couldn't help but smile as I complimented him, I had never come across anyone like him before and I stood and walked over to the piano. Again I felt awkward, uncomfortable as he sat in silence, his eyes following me as I walked the long walk. I shifted and squirmed as I stood next to the piano and without warning he lunged at me and grabbed at the belt of the robe. He looked up at me with those beautiful devilish eyes and pulled me towards him, pushing me against the keys of the piano. His hard stare moved down to my body as he pulled at the belt allowing it to fall open. I stood frozen in shock and anticipation as he ran his fingers over my stiff nipples and cupped my breasts. He lingered there for a second or two as I tried hard to control my breathing. His hands moved down to my navel as his eyes appeared to soften and he leaned into me so that our lips were barely millimetres apart.

"Last night was amazing," he whispered.

I nodded gently, unable to form any words as my breathing increased. His hands were around my waist as he pulled me towards him and he started to kiss me hard. His mouth kissed my cheeks and then my neck and then he took one of my nipples in his mouth as he sucked hard.

My God it was happening all over again and the slightest touch from this man had me in raptures. I put my arms around his neck; perhaps he was interested after all?

I could feel the energy course through my veins as he moved to my other breast and I summoned the courage to weave my hands inside his robe as I slid it over his shoulders and lifted my leg over him poised, ready, barely inches away from his rapidly stiffening cock. He smiled a wicked grin as he held my hips firmly in place preventing me from getting any lower. He knew I wanted him so much and yet he needed to be in control and I knew it. I melted in his arms like a limp rag doll as he threw my naked backside against the piano keys as I searched behind me for something to hang on to. He eased his body forward and reached for his hard cock and eased slowly inside me. I lifted my legs and wrapped them around his back as he thrust hard into me.

It was almost comical as he picked up pace and the key pads banged out an undistinguishable tune. I felt the heat flowing through my body as I could feel him getting harder inside me. He reached for my hands and pinned them flat on the surface of the piano behind me as he continued to force himself deeper and deeper inside me. His tongue was forceful and firm as he continued to kiss me and I could feel myself getting more and more turned on. I fought to free my hands, convinced I would lose my balance and crash onto the floor. Then his fingers were inside me pushing hard and deep inside me.

"Oh my God, stop," I said as his pace increased and he stopped momentarily, watching me with that wicked grin before removing his fingers. He reached for his cock and eased himself inside me.

"How about this?" he said. "Do you want me to stop this?" he demanded.

I groaned, still trying to free my wrists.

"Ask me to stop and I will, just tell me to stop Jess."

"No," I moaned, "don't stop please."

"Why shouldn't I stop?"

"It feels too good," I said, defeated.

"I can see it does," he whispered, releasing my wrists allowing me to wrap them around his neck as I kissed him gently probing into his mouth with my tongue as he quickened up again and his thrusts got harder and deeper.

"Fucking hell," he cried out as I felt him filling me as his hard cock swelled towards a climax.

That wicked grin as he pulled out yet again and yet I loved every second.

"Ladies first."

He grinned, kissing me again as his finger searched expertly for my clit. I moaned into his mouth as he kissed me hard and worked me up to the point of no return. He knew exactly what he was doing as he measured my climax to the second and as I arched my back and my whole body tensed up he slipped his cock back inside me thrusting hard into me bringing me to the most intense orgasm I'd ever known and we cried out together in unison as he came too in an orgasm that seemed to last longer than I could ever remember.

He was panting hard, his face a perfect sheen of perspiration as he collapsed onto the floor taking me with him as we lay laughing together.

"I'm sorry," he said, "my legs are completely shot, I couldn't hold that position any longer."

We lay in silence as he stroked my hair as we lay side by side and our breathing eventually returned to normal. This was different, something I had never experienced before and something I wanted to last forever.

But it didn't. My phone buzzed bringing us back to reality.

"Is that yours?" he asked.

"Yes I should probably check it; I'm supposed to be meeting my Mum later."

I was lying through my teeth. I actually had a session later that afternoon, a session where I would be playing the part of a brash, blond bitch which involved a trip to the high street showing no mercy to my client's credit cards. My God, what if I should bump into Edward, what if he found out about my secret life?

I currently had no idea of the time, I felt as if I were hyperventilating, I needed to get out of there because in an instant I had remembered what it was I did to pay the bills, to put a roof over my head and I knew it wasn't conventional and within a twelve hour period something had happened in my life that I just couldn't handle, something that I had not been prepared for. Was I falling in love?

I almost ran back into the bedroom slipped on my damaged underwear and pulled last night's dress over my head suddenly realising I had to do the walk of shame. You've been there. There are certain shoes and certain clothes you only wear for a night out and as you walk to the taxi rank or down the high street you know that everyone who looks at you realises you have been on your back most of the night with a man you've probably only just met.

Checking my phone there were two emails from my client asking for confirmation for the appointment. I quickly typed a reply and slipped the phone back in my bag. Edward was staring at me again.

I walked back into the lounge.

"I should probably call a cab," I murmured; trying not to blush. Please don't let this be awkward I thought.

"Don't be silly," he said. "Andrew can drop you back home."

"Honestly, there is no need," I replied, not sure if I wanted his driver dropping me home.

I didn't want him to know where I lived and wondered how many other girls his driver took home in the space of an average month.

Edward was looking at me, his head slightly tilted.

"Why are you frowning, is it something I've said."

I hadn't realised that I was probably looking a little upset but yes, I was. My thoughts of how many of Edward's one night stands got to use the chauffeur was obviously pissing me off and it was showing.

I tried to shake it off.

"No, I'm fine," I lied, thinking that I did want to use the chauffeur because it would cancel out the walk of shame that I really didn't want to do.

At least he knew what had happened last night and God forbid, it would be just my luck if I got a cab and the driver was someone I knew.

"If it's not too much trouble that would be great."

"Good. I'll call him now," he said. He walked through to the bedroom and came back through to the lounge wearing some expensive looking tracksuit bottoms and a t-shirt.

"Also he will know where you live, so there is no escaping me," he laughed.

I wondered if this was a positive sign. Perhaps he does want to see me again.

Edward was texting.

"He will be downstairs in five minutes," he said walking towards me. "Can I see you again, dinner tonight maybe?"

Shit! I was caught off guard, so this wasn't a one nighter then. He did actually want to see me again.

I tried to play it cool.

"I've got a really busy day, but yes if I can manage it I guess, yes that would be nice."

I smiled trying not to gush.

"Great, say eightish? Andrew and I can pick you up and I'll be able to have a few glasses of champagne."

I nodded. I nodded and grinned like the over excited schoolgirl I tried so desperately hard not to be and it was written all over my face that this was the best thing that had happened to me in a long long time.

Edward leaned into me and gave me a long lingering kiss. He took my hand and led me towards the door. My hand felt so good in his and we kissed again as the lift took us down to the ground floor. Andrew was waiting and Edward gave me a small peck on the cheek as he said goodbye. He firmed up the evenings arrangements with Andrew and I was gone.

In the car I messaged my client back and confirmed our late afternoon meeting. It had just gone twelve thirty so I had plenty of time to get Russell, take him for a walk and get ready for the hour long session.

My phone buzzed, it was Edward.

'Can't wait to see you later Jessica xxx'

My heart skipped a beat; he was perfect and I felt like I was walking on air.

Chapter Ten

I had another lucrative session on the high street. I humiliated my client in Debenhams, two designer shops and the best jewellers in town where he bought a four hundred pound necklace on his credit card. I acted well; but it was difficult to keep up the charade because all I was thinking about was Edward and how special he was. I was always looking over my shoulder, paranoid and petrified that he would walk into where I was and recognise me.

I half expected my client to complain that I hadn't been up to scratch but he didn't. He gave me a sweet sickly smile and gave me a hundred pounds by way of a tip as he disappeared into the department store toilets to relieve himself. I'm not quite sure how long his self-pleasuring session lasted because I left before he came back. I couldn't wait to get away, couldn't wait to get out of my tarts' clothes, take a shower and get rid of the character that was Mistress Zeta. As I applied my make-up ready for the big night I was wondering if it were possible to combine a normal relationship with a wholly abnormal profession where I humiliate and take money from men.

Business was going great which was exactly what I needed to take my mind of Edward and yet was it? The more clients I got and the more money I earned the deeper I fell into a pit that I couldn't get out of. I worked from home online around three days a week seeing customers from abroad and British guys who didn't want to meet me. I found this interesting; they were happy to pay around one hundred pounds for a half hour session over Skype and indulge in their kinky submissive side. This was fine by me and I came to the conclusion that in their mind if they ever met me in person everything would become a reality. Being online it was easier to push this part of their life to the back of their minds and forget it had ever happened. I understood and fully respected their wishes and of course I've no doubt that most of them were probably married and of course everyone is entitled to their privacy. I also saw on average two or three men face to face each week and the money and the gifts poured in. At one point my earnings (including gifts bought on credit cards) peaked at nearly five thousand pounds per week, where else could I earn that sort of money?

The requests I was receiving on email were pushing the boundaries more and more. Some of them I would be willing to do, those that were fun anyway and I can tell you sometimes I fought hard to stop breaking out into a fit of the giggles as I did what was asked of me. I switched on the laptop a few days after my dinner date with Edward and watched as emails from the last forty eight hours loaded. A few lunch humiliation sessions, a Skype booking and well an email that not only shocked me but again made me realise that in the fetish world there are no limits.

"Dear Mistress,

I have wanted to approach you for a long time now with my fantasy. For some time now I have wanted you to own me totally, I want you to take me as your pet, your plaything, everything I have rightfully belongs to you. I would pray to the Gods you read on and consider my request for an eventual face to face session. My fantasy is that I serve you for a few months over Skype. I want you to take complete control of me and I will fall deeper under your spell giving you whatever you want. In a bid to impress you I hint about my financial status and the fact my mortgage is nearly paid off. Over time you work on me and constantly ask when I will have the deeds to my house. Foolishly I tell you the date but I realise you do not have my personal details and so think I am safe. I am wrong; you have been grooming me and know my name from the online payments. Within a small while you obtain my address in a bid to take my little lasting freedom. One night there is a knock at my door. I usually ignore cold callers but the knock was accompanied by a text coming through on my phone. 'Knock knock' it says, 'who's there little piggy: is it you?'

I sneak to the window and see a BMW or similar car parked outside and two slim figures stood at my door. I realise one of them is you and I run not knowing what to do, I am in shock!

I hear your voices as you call through the letterbox when I suddenly remember that I have not locked the door. I start to panic, realising you will very shortly try the handle and let yourself in. As I process this terrifying thought I hear your stilettos on the wood floor as you both enter.

'Here piggy piggy', you call laughing to your friend.

'Come on Sara, let's have a look around this place, I want to see what I will get for it, it looks a fair size."

I hide in the airing cupboard, petrified as you walk around down stairs taking notes.

I hear you shouting.

"I'm coming up piggy and I will find you."

I nearly stop breathing, I have nowhere to go and I know it will be a matter of minutes before you find me but despite this feeling of being trapped by you I'm totally aroused. Your footsteps become louder as you both climb the wooden stairs laughing at my misfortune! As I try to keep still in amongst the towels and bed sheets, my breathing is hard and my dick even harder. I watch the shadow at the bottom of the door as you pass by towards the bedroom.

"I know you're up here wanker, let's see, you're probably under the bed or in a closet of some sort."

You cackle like a witch and I let out a whimper as you finish the sentence. I hear you in my bedroom and the sound of papers rustling.

"Well well, what do we have here Sara? I do believe I have found the deeds to this little old mansion of his." You laugh again. "The stupid prick left them on his little desk, how funny, come on Sara lets go downstairs and discuss this sale."

You walk by the closet I am hiding in as if you know I am there. "And you Wanker will come and meet us downstairs. If you don't come down I will personally come and drag you there myself you annoying little fuck."

As you walk back along the hallway I open the cupboard door slightly to see your beautiful blonde hair as you descend the stairs. A few moments later I appear in the sitting room, I refrain from looking at you, afraid but also immensely aroused.

"Get on your knees in my company, you cretin," you say.

I follow your orders to the letter and listen to your conversation with the estate agent. I listen to how you will lease my property immediately whilst it is up for sale. I crawl on my knees to you asking permission to be heard.

"Be quiet piggy and drink this." You smile as you pass me a wine glass.

"That's it, drink up there's a good piggy."

Your smile is poison as I do what I'm told. I suddenly feel so strange, the room spins as I listen to you tell Sara that you have plans for me. I crawl around on the floor desperate for the room to stop spinning. The last thing I hear before I black out is that I will now be kept as your rent boy ready to entertain wealthy clients with discreet services. I awake finding myself naked and tied up in the boot of your car. I have been captured, taken and now I am yours. You will do as you wish with me for as long as you see fit.

That Mistress, is my fantasy. Please tell me this can happen Mistress, please. I would love so much to be yours.

Yours faithfully
Reg"

I kid you not this guy actually thought I would be able to do this. And whilst I'm always looking to take on a new client and push the boundaries, well, even to me this was just fucked up and I had no intention of following this one through.

Knowing my luck it would be a set up and I would get done for breaking and entering, possibly even a kidnapping charge. Hmm... I'll have to pass on this one. I chuckled to myself and closed the laptop shut as a text from Edward came through on my mobile.

'Can't wait for later darling, pick you up at eight tonight, we have something to discuss.'

Shit! What did he mean we have something to discuss? Things were going well, or at least they seemed to be so what did we need to talk about? I refilled my coffee cup whilst trying not to panic then it dawned on me; he had asked a few times where I worked as he knew I wasn't a dancer like Summer. I think I told him I was working as a waitress in a restaurant but what had Summer said to her date? And had her date spilled the beans? Summer knew I was dabbling with the online dominatrix side of things but Jesus Christ surely she hadn't told anyone. That was it, it had to be. Edward had found out I had lied and he was going to question me about the restaurant I supposedly worked in and where it was and shit! He might even want to suggest going there tonight.

My God I was now in an almighty panic. Would I have to tell him the truth and if I did why would he possibly want to go out with a girl who abuses men for a living? I had that empty feeling in the pit of my stomach, I really liked him and it was about to come crashing down to earth, I just knew it.

I got ready for the evenings date with Edward. I was a bundle of nerves continuously rehearsing what I was going to say about my current job role. I found myself wondering if what I was doing was wrong. I knew it wasn't quite normal but I wasn't having sex and I wasn't selling myself either. But with this looming conversation hanging over me I wondered about lying, about blagging it that Summer had just been winding his friend up and that I was really a nice normal girl.

Forty minutes before the car was due to pick me up I decided that I was going to be honest. I would hammer home the point that there was no sexual contact with my clients and it was really just a step away from being a counsellor or a shrink and who knows maybe he would be ok with it?

I chose what I was going to wear carefully and eventually went for my new thigh-high Jimmy Choo boots and a silk shirt dress with a thin gold belt that hung loosely around my waist. I was ready a good fifteen minutes early which was very unusual for me and stood by the door rehearsing the speech which would undoubtedly come.

He picked me up one minute before eight pm. I was immediately on the back foot because Andrew wasn't with him and of course I read the worst into the scenario convinced he was going to start quizzing me immediately. I slid nervously into the passenger seat of his Porsche and he appeared to scan me from top to bottom.

"You're looking rather sinful tonight," he smirked as he bit his lip.

Perhaps I had gone a bit over the top but I was dressed to impress just in case the shit hit the fan and I wanted to know that I was looking at my best to keep my confidence high. Perhaps I was stupid enough to think that he wouldn't want to let me go if he liked what he saw. Does that make sense?

As we started driving out to the country I was going over in my mind what I was going to say. We talked about nothing at first, about food and how hungry we were and he mentioned that he could leave his car at the restaurant and Andrew would collect us meaning Edward could have some wine with dinner. As we started to talk about the weather my defences were gradually coming down and then all of a sudden he changed the subject, came out with it – straight and to the point and caught me off guard.

"You haven't been strictly honest with me Jess. My friend told me that him and Summer had a very interesting conversation about what you do for a living."

Shit! Summer... I'll kill her. He was staring straight ahead at the road while he was speaking and I wanted to turn and look at him but I was scared witless and even though it was dark I sensed that if we did make eye contact he would gage how acutely uncomfortable I was.

"You work in the sex industry don't you?"

"No!" I almost shouted. "I most certainly do not."

I was genuinely angry at the suggestion and yet, yes of course I worked in the sex industry but the mere mention of it suggested I was some sort of whore.

Edward still focused on the road as he spoke in a monotone, unemotional voice. "Summer said you were a dominatrix. That sounds like the sex industry to me, a dominatrix dominates men sexually is that not the case?"

"Yes... err no, I mean."

Fuck, I wasn't thinking straight, this wasn't how it was supposed to pan out and my tongue was in knots.

"Yes," I stuttered. "I'm sort of a dominatrix, nothing sexual. On my part I mean, I um see a lot of guys over the web and we Skype and I never meet them and I don't even have to take my clothes off, but well, I , some of them..."

"Calm down Jessica, I'm only asking," he said, "and we haven't even been out on a proper date yet so I'm not your keeper but I like you and I figured if you had to lie to me then you must be ashamed of what you do."

"No, well not exactly but then again I don't feel like broadcasting it and I certainly wouldn't be happy telling my mother what I do."

I turned to look at him. Did I spot a trace of a smile? I continued. "You've no idea how many warped fantasies are out there Edward. If I told you, you simply wouldn't believe me."

"I'm not interested," he said. "If you don't have sex with them or touch them in any way then I can handle that but you shouldn't have lied that's all I'm saying Jessica."

Jesus Christ why was I feeling like a schoolgirl in the headmaster's office?

He turned to look at me briefly.

"You don't have any sexual contact do you?"

"No. no I've never had sex for money it's not what you might think Edward, and I wanted to tell you, I just..."

He cut in.

"I know you're a strong girl Jess but I'm a traditional man when it comes to who wears the trousers in a relationship, understand that. I take it you make good money, and I must say I am relieved you no longer dance, that would have been a problem for me almost certainly."

He placed his hand on my knee.

"I like you Jessica, you know that."

His Porsche sped along the dark road as I sensed a change of tone in his voice.

"I like you too." I beamed over at him.

This was going better than I thought.

"But you must remember what I have just said; I am a very traditional man."

He took his eyes off the road temporarily as he stared at me and slid his hand up my thigh. He took me by surprise as he located my lace panties and I parted my legs slightly almost instinctively.

"That goes for the bedroom too Jess, don't get any ideas because if I so desire I'll fuck you within an inch of your life."

Well, let me say no man has ever talked to me that way and my immediate reaction was to tell him to back off. I was a strong girl so who did he think he was speaking to in that tone? But I didn't. In fact I almost melted into the seat as I eased back and said nothing moving my legs further apart to give him the access he wanted.

"Remember how I pursued you? Hunted you and trapped you in the cubicle?"

His fingers pulled the lace to the side as he felt for me and slid a single finger deep inside me as I tensed up and caught my breath.

"I take it you do remember Jessica, don't you?"

I was conscious of the car slowing down which I was more than grateful for.

"Take them off now or I'll fucking rip them off."

Oh Jesus! Where was this coming from? Edward was changing down through the gears and I did exactly as I was told as I lifted my knees and slid my G-string off dropping it into the well of the car.

He pulled off into a bumpy layby and turned the engine off.

"Out!" he ordered as he reached over and opened my door. I climbed out without a murmur of protest. He walked slowly but purposely round to the passenger side and unzipped his trousers as he let them fall onto the ground. He gave me a quick peck on the lips then grabbed my wrist as he spun me around and threw me forcefully against the car door. He grabbed my ponytail, yanking my head to the side with his free hand and he kissed me hard. He tasted minty with a faint smell of his expensive aftershave. He held my jaw as his hand left my hair as he traced it down my back. I was helpless and at the same time petrified in case someone showed up and yet I knew there and then that whatever he did to me I wouldn't resist.

He reached the hem of my dress and slipped his hand underneath as he grabbed roughly at my backside. I could feel his hardness pushing against me as I fought hard to control my breathing.

I was panicking.

"What if someone comes?" I gasped.

His fingers found my wetness again.

"The only person coming will be me," he mocked as felt his hard cock pushing slowly into me.

"Remember what I said," he growled as he thrust hard into me and I gasped as he forced my whole body against the cold steel of the car.

The feeling was exquisite and despite my overwhelming panic I closed my eyes and accepted that there was no escape. I didn't want to escape the pleasure enveloping my whole body as my hips banged against the car door. I was immensely turned on but getting booked for indecent exposure was not in the plans.

I begged him to be quick. He could take me if he insisted and it was turning me on so much but Jesus make it quick before anyone comes along. So the bastard slowed right down just to confirm to me that he was in control and there was nothing I could do about it. If Edward wanted this fuck to last an hour then that's precisely how long it would last. He thrust into me deeper and harder leaving go of my jaw and kissing my neck softly and incredibly I started to relax.

Fuck it, I thought, fuck it. This was incredible sex, spontaneous, daring and I loved it and all of a sudden my thoughts drifted to the pleasure coursing through me and I didn't want it to stop and if the entire Metropolitan Police Force turned up en masse I'd shout over to them that they had permission to watch but for God's sake don't interrupt.

"Go to the bonnet," he murmured as he released me. I moved around to the bonnet without questioning him as he followed me. I was facing him now and he kissed me slowly, his tongue slipping seductively between my teeth as I bit gently into it. Suddenly he grabbed my waist, spun me around roughly and pulled my dress up to my hips exposing my bare backside to the early summer breeze. I knew exactly what was coming as he pushed me face down onto the sleek bonnet of the car, spread my legs and entered me again. My God! The excitement and the thrill of being caught was adding to my pleasure as his hard cock pounded into me. Within a minute it was all too much for me as that familiar feeling started to rapidly rise through my body.

"Don't stop!" I screamed out as I neared that wonderful rush.

"Tell me you want it Jess. Ask me for it!" he ordered.

"Fuck me hard," I stammered. "Please."

Edward was close to climax too, I could sense it as my dirty demand seemed to heighten his senses and he quickened up. He was breathing hard and he had leaned forward so that I could now feel his hot breath on the back of my neck as his cock swelled hard inside me. He leaned back again as he started moaning and with his large hand he gave me a couple of hard slaps on my backside. It tipped me over the edge sending me in one of the most sensational orgasms I had ever had. A second or two later Edward cried out as he came to.

"Don't ever forget who the boss is," he whispered as we lay face first on the warm bonnet.

As our breathing returned to normal he stood back, pulled my dress down and presented me with my lace panties.

"I believe these are yours darling," he said. "Now come on we will be late for dinner."

"Are you crazy?" I said. "I'm a lady and I'm hot, sweaty and dirty and my make-up is all over my face! If you think I'm in any condition to sit down at the table of some fancy restaurant then you are very much mistaken."

He stood for a second or two and sort of shrugged his shoulders as if to say why not? Then he took a real good look at me and burst out laughing.

"I suppose you do look a little dishevelled," he said.

"Dishevelled?"

"Okay, but I'm hungry," he said. "I'll pick up an Indian or a Chinese and we can go back to mine. You can take a quick shower and I'll open some wine."

As we slid back into the car and sped off, the conversation of how I earned my living was not mentioned again that evening. I did indeed shower and we had a beautiful Indian meal and shared a decent Spanish Rioja. Afterwards we made love again, this time a little more gently and I fell asleep in my lover's arms, happy and content. In fact I was feeling better than I ever had in my life. Now I knew for certain I was in love and I was enjoying every minute.

Life was indescribably good. I was looking forward to my week ahead. While Edward hadn't actually given me his blessing on what it was I did for a living the fact that he still couldn't seem to get enough of me was a kind of an approval, or at least that's what I told myself.

I was busy with new customers all wanting to feel my wrath and the money was rolling in. My client base was building and I was now only dealing with the men I was comfortable with. I didn't need to watch them jacking off in their own vomit as they force fed themselves sandwiches and yet I was more than comfortable flinging a few hundred custard pies at a naked man. I knew I had to meet new clients in the hope that one day I could find utopia, twenty easy clients who were mega rich and wanted a dom once a month and their own particular fetish wasn't so perverted that it upset me. I was growing to respect many of my clients, realising that deep down they were harmless and perfectly normal but with slightly unconventional sexual tastes. Even the sandwich man didn't offend me or worry me too much, he was harmless in his own sort of way but I'm afraid he did make me a little queasy and that's why he had to be blocked.

I've been asked several times by my girlfriends how I look upon my clients. For example do I feel sorry for them, do I understand their needs or do I look down on them as depraved perverts? I wouldn't ever say that, and it's each to their own and what is normal anyway? The world is changing; attitudes are changing too. Even now, in some parts of the world such as Yemen, Iran and Nigeria, homosexual and extramarital practices are punishable by death. I find that extraordinary and it just goes to show the differing attitudes to sexual preferences expressed around the globe and in different cultures and religions, so who am I to say a man who gets turned on wallowing naked in shaving foam is worse than the next man?

I wouldn't even consider trying to describe normality but I remember a quote I once read somewhere. It went something like: 'The only people we can think of as normal are those we don't yet know very well".

I think that just about sums it up.

Chapter Eleven

I had a meeting with a man down from Scotland on business wanting to go on a shopping trip. He said he wanted to be left with no money. Not a penny he said and I had to abuse him from the outset. It sounded like fun, an okay job and lucrative too so I replied to the email and arranged to meet him. I got ready and made my way to the pre-arranged meeting place. He came pacing through the crowded street with a wheelie suitcase. Oh my God he was pitiful and I noticed straight away.

He strode purposely up to me.

"Oh Mistress, or Goddess, please can I call you goddess?" he panted, beads of perspiration standing out on his over high forehead. He was so tall I had to tilt my head right back just to look at him.

Time for the act to begin.

"Are you fucking kidding me, the suitcase? Are we really going around all the shops with your fucking luggage."

"I'm so sorry," he stammered. "I will be going straight to the airport afterwards, I'm sorry, I'm sorry."

"Oh for God's sake," I sighed, "come on then."

I turned quickly on my heels and marched off leaving the giant Scotsman walking behind me knocking people out of the way as his stupid suitcase clattered into a dozen ankle bones. He was so damn big, no one said a word to him.

First stop was the perfume store. He led me there, and he had obviously done his homework.

"I know you wear Chanel Goddess," he blushed.

I turned and smirked at him.

"Oh really? A fan are we loser?"

"Oh yes Mistress, I love you I think about you all the time," he whispered as he came a little closer.

"Well that's not a bit creepy is it?" I took a step back. "And stop standing so close your breath smells."

"I'm sorry Goddess; please may I buy you some Coco Mademoiselle? I know it's one of your favourites too, I also know you love Dior makeup."

He pointed over to the Dior counter catching the attention of a snooty sales girl caked in inch thick cosmetics.

I was already tiring of him and this was only the first shop. Still, this was work I told myself, this was another girls nine to five, another girls Tesco check-out desk but at least I was working on a slightly higher rate. I stared at him for a good twenty seconds as I watched his discomfort growing.

"Yes you can buy me some perfume but calm down and try and relax, buy me some Coco Mademoiselle and we will head to a lingerie store but stop making a bloody exhibition of yourself will you?"

"Yes Goddess."

The lady behind the Chanel stand was now sweetly smiling.

"Can I help?" she drawled in a fake posh voice.

"Yes please," I said. "The largest bottle of Coco Mademoiselle you have and he's paying."

"Certainly Madam," she said. "We have a 100ml bottle at a hundred and nineteen pounds. Would that be acceptable?"

I turned my nose up and stared at the Scotsman and then looked back at Miss Snooty.

"Have you nothing bigger?"

She shook her head.

"Okay," I said, "that will do for now."

I pointed at the now beetroot faced pig, told the assistant he was paying by credit card and walked off.

Approximately five minutes later he scurried over wheeling his case carrying the first purchase.

"Oh shit Mistress she knows, she knows I'm your loser."

He was going into full melt down and enjoying every second as he scanned the shop floor.

"I... I... oh my God everyone is looking at me."

I took a quick look around. There was literally no one in the large department store. What drugs was he on?

I milked the situation.

"Okay piggy calm the fuck down."

I leaned into him and gripped him by the jaw forcing his head to scan a one eighty.

"The store is empty you idiot."

I was trying not to laugh.

"Look around." I turned in a full circle with my arms out. "Look. No one here, not a soul, just a Goddess and one big screwed up loser."

"Oh, yes, yes you're right," he spluttered out, looking around the empty store. "I get a little carried away thinking people are watching me and realise I'm a pay pig. I'm sorry Mistress, err Goddess."

Was he the one acting now? I knew he was enjoying every second of the experience, his email told me that this was exactly what he had wanted and yet here he was telling me he was embarrassed in front of an empty store.

"Okay listen," I said sternly, "even if there were anyone here they would just assume you were my poor downtrodden boyfriend trying to make it up to me because you've fucked up somewhere along the line.

He looked around the store yet again and then smiled at me. Fuck, I could have punched that smile from his face in an instance.

"Oh I would love it if they thought I was your boyfriend."

I shrugged my shoulders.

"Whatever piggy."

"Yes, yes, well let's move on shall we?" he said. "I'm sorry Mistress."

"Are we composed?" I asked raising an eyebrow.

"Yes, so sorry Goddess, I mean Mistress."

As we went up the escalator I told him what we were about to do. "I have a boyfriend, obviously, and you're going to choose underwear for him okay?"

"Yes Mistress."

"It has to be sexy, seductive and you need to be aware that he will fuck me in it later on tonight, is that clear?"

"Holy shit Mistress," he blurted out catching the attention of a woman and her little boy travelling down the escalator opposite us, she scowled and looked me up and down using her hands like earmuffs on the kid's ears. I smiled in an apologetic manner as the pig – totally clueless – listed the colours of lingerie he would love to buy. Oh my God I was drained and I still had about an hour and a half left. He was literally zapping my energy leaving a trail of disruption in our wake. Get a grip Jess, I told myself, this little job could net a grand's worth of quality pressies if you get your act together.

So I spent over ninety pounds on some nice underwear while I forced him to examine them in front of a clearly uncomfortable sales lady. He squirmed and apologised profusely to me and the assistant during the time it took to process the transaction. As I left the store, two shopping bags safely on board I suddenly had a wicked idea.

"Where to next?" he said.

"Well, you know my boyfriend is very highly sexed and oh so wicked."

His bottom lip trembled. He knew exactly what was coming.

"Ann Summers," I announced.

"Oh no Mistress, I simply couldn't, it would be more than-"

I took a firm hold of his pathetic cheap tie and twisted.

"You'll go wherever I want is that clear you snivelling pathetic little creature?"

"Yes Mistress."

"Excellent," I replied with a grin. "Ann Summers it is."

I walked away as he followed on behind me like a little lost sheep.

We spent about forty five minutes in Ann Summers and I drove him insane. I swear he nearly broke down in tears on three or four occasions. He drove me insane too though, thank God, I managed to get a little time alone in the dressing room before I went totally mad.

"Go and pay," I said shoving an armful of corsets and provocative outfits at him.

"Now fuck off will you?" He was trying to poke his head through the curtain of the changing room as I pushed him away.

He was standing at the till when I left the changing room. What a sight he was with his trusty little wheelie case by his side. At this stage I decided to have some fun at his expense. I stood by him as he fumbled with his credit card in the machine and smiled as it took him three attempts to get his pin number right. He finished and put the card in his wallet as he turned to face me.

"What are you doing?"

He looked at me all confused.

"We're leaving aren't we?" he said.

"Are we hell? I haven't even started."

And I walked over to the far side of the store knowing that he would be following in my wake. I stood by the bondage section eyeing up the handcuffs, paddles, whips and nipple clamps. I took a leather restraining gag from the shelf and turned to face him.

"Do you know what this is?" I asked.

"No Mistress."

I waved it in front of his face.

"Let's just say it would have come in extremely handy if I'd had this in my possession two hours ago."

"Sorry Mistress."

So I collected one of the little net baskets they have in Ann Summers and I started to buy. I bought some of the handcuffs and a Rampant Rabbit while he whimpered and begged me to stop threatening to leave the store which of course I knew he never would. I bought some special toys for couples and then spied some vibrating cock rings. He was genuinely puzzled when I placed it in his hand.

"What is it?" he said.

I shook my head. "You really don't know do you?"

"No Mistress."

So I explained.

"My boyfriend has a huge cock and this should fit him just perfectly. As he's screwing me this vibrates on my clitoris sending me into raptures. (Cue sniffling and whimpering) Have you ever sent a girl into raptures?"

"No Mistress."

I placed the device into my basket.

"I thought not, but let me tell you that sometime this evening my boyfriend will be doing just that and you piggy will be paying for the privilege."

"Yes Mistress."

And then I spotted it, a man's cock cage on a shelf aptly named 'chastity devices'. It was stainless steel in the shape of a small cock with a ring at the top and a padlock. I had no idea what it did but it looked made to measure for my piggy and cost fifty pounds. I picked it up.

"Now this looks right up your street."

"No Mistress please, I can't buy that I won't buy that," he sniffed.

I stood with my hands on my hips.

"What did you say?"

He didn't move, he didn't say a word and I placed it into the basket as I walked towards the till. He caught up with me half way across the shop.

"Mistress, please, wait."

"What is it?"

"Will you stamp on my foot?"

"What?" I said totally shocked.

He repeated his warped request.

"Will you stamp on my foot, please? When I pay, will you do that for me? I would love that."

He was practically salivating looking at the thin stiletto on my ankle boot.

"That looks like it would really hurt," he panted.

"Let me get this right," I said. "You want me to stamp on your foot while you pay for these things?"

He was nodding with a sick grin on his face.

"Hard," he said.

I'm sure you are reading this thinking the author is using more than a little poetic licence and exaggerating this story for effect but I swear blind that I am not. I was standing in a sex shop with a stranger with everything you could ever imagine of a sexual nature within touching distance and yet he wanted nothing more than for me to stamp on his foot with a sharp stiletto heel.

I looked down at my heel. The shoes were well made, this would hurt him more than he realised.

"Are you sure?"

"Yes Mistress."

"Fine," I muttered wondering what sort of crazy this man was. We walked to the counter and I placed the basket on top.

"Um I'd, uh, I'd like to buy these please," he stuttered looking at the floor.

I reached into the basket and pulled out the little cock cage and spoke to the assistant.

"Can you believe he gets a thrill out of wearing one of these?"

The poor girl didn't know where to look but came back with a well-rehearsed line.

"Who are we to judge? We all have our little secrets."

Well said, I thought to myself, but you wouldn't begin to understand my secrets if I was to share them with you.

The loser looked up from the floor quickly as if to give me a cue so I went for it as the assistant reached for the basket. I delicately put my heel slap bang in the middle of his foot and shifted all my weight onto it. I could see his fists clench as I did so, convinced he was about to let out a squeal as the stiletto stabbed through the thin canvas of his cheap shoes and ground into flesh and sinew before stopping as it reached hard bone. My God, I felt it myself and as I eventually lifted my foot up and removed it the relief in his eyes was clearly visible.

"I'll be outside, hurry up," I smirked, disappearing quickly.

He took some time and I as waited for him I checked my phone. I was expecting a message from Edward but there was nothing. I had a wicked thought; I could surprise him this evening and turn up in my new lingerie. Mmm now there's a thought. I grinned to myself as I stared off in to space, quickly brought down with a bump as the clumsy Scotsman stumbled limping out of the shop clutching the bags and of course his bloody suitcase.

"Oh my God that was amazing Mistress," his voice dropped to a whisper as he came even closer.

"I nearly came Mistress."

"Really?"

I stared up at him in amazement. What the hell could possibly be going through his head right now I wondered, as he stood there red and sweaty with a damaged foot. I looked down at his shoe and sure enough a little blood had seeped through his sock and onto the surface of the shoe.

I moved in for the kill with not an ounce of sympathy left in my body.

"Okay pig, empty your wallet and pockets, I'm under strict instruction to take every penny you've got before you get on that plane."

He looked worried, this always happens. Whenever it comes to the crunch they get cold feet, but it's what they ask me to do and without fail when I carry out their instructions to the letter (as I was doing now) they contact me to say they are so glad I carried out their wishes.

"Empty them NOW!" I demanded.

The loser reluctantly dug into his pocket and took out his wallet. I snatched it out of his hand before he had a chance to open it. I counted the notes.

"One hundred and twenty quid, is that it? For fuck's sake. I've spent more than that on a decent bottle of wine."

I stood for a second or two and watched him on the verge of tears.

"Empty your fucking pockets or I'll empty them for you, you loser."

He blushed as he looked at the people walking by and I almost thought he was about to refuse. But he didn't. He reached into the inside pockets of his jacket and pulled out a few twenties and a couple of ten pound notes. I urged him on and he dug into his jeans, took out a few coins and three crumpled note.

I clicked my fingers and opened my hand.

"Give it here loser."

"Yes Mistress."

He shoved it into my hand and then looked at me.

"One more shop Mistress, let me buy you something else."

I looked longingly at my watch.

"I have to be going soon."

"Please Mistress no, just a few more shops."

"No!" I said. "I've only got time for one more shop and you can buy me a dress there, then I'll have to go."

I was getting irritated, I really wanted to get away from him but I hadn't yet made my target.

"Come on, we'll have to be quick, I've got a social life unlike you."

I walked off as he started to plead again.

"Listen," I spat, "if you start to cause a scene I'm leaving straight away, understand? You're a grown man, pull yourself together for fuck's sake."

He sulked as I turned and walked away but I heard him follow on behind me as I crossed the road and headed for the boutique opposite.

"Idiot!" I muttered to myself and this time I wasn't acting, I was getting sick of his demands by the second. God, I can't wait to call and surprise Edward and relax with a nice long steamy session.

"Come on tosser," I called as he dragged his injured foot behind him trying to waste time.

In the boutique I found a lovely lace dress and tried it on showing him what it looked like, teasing him by telling him it would only be on for a few minutes when I went to my boyfriend's later in the day.

He put his card in the machine and it registered at one hundred and fifty one pounds. It took me by surprise as I hadn't even looked at the price tag. We went outside and I couldn't wait to get away from him.

"Now I must dash and you piggy have a plane to catch."

He was off again, begging me to stay and go to just one more shop but I flatly refused. He eventually realised I was having none of it.

"Please wait, okay no more shops but before you go stamp on my foot again."

We were now standing in the busy street and I was getting truly pissed off.

"No I have to go," I replied sternly.

"Please, please," he begged as his big sad eyes started to well up.

"You've got to be joking me, we have a crier in the middle of the high street because he's not getting what he wants."

The tears had started to fall on his cheeks now.

"Please stamp on me," he begged, whimpering.

"That's it, give me the bags please, I have to go."

I lunged at them and snatched them before this could get any more embarrassingly awkward. I was wrong; a large snot bubble erupted from his nostril as he started to sob quietly pleading for one last stamp. I didn't know what else to do so I turned quickly and started walking away but he had grabbed my jacket and I was rooted to the spot.

I panicked momentarily, realising that this well-built powerful man could pose a real danger.

"Let go now or I will scream."

I stared at him coldly but still he held on tightly. Instinct then took over as I gripped his wrist and tried to break free. He was having none of it so I raised my foot and powered it into his metatarsal bone. I was aware of the sickening crack almost immediately, as he sank slowly to the ground in agony.

"My God," I whispered. "What have I done?"

The Scotsman was turning grey as he lay in a heap on the pavement and suddenly I became aware of a small crowd gathering around us.

"What is it?" someone said, "has he had a heart attack? Call an ambulance."

Well, would you believe it? The next time I looked at the Scotsman I swear I noticed a flicker of a smile on his face. He was telling everyone to leave him alone as he had a plane to catch but the blood was pouring from his shoe. He had spotted a pharmacy across the road and asked the Good Samaritans to help him over. I stood rooted to the spot as two burly blokes lifted him up and carried him over the road. As he disappeared through the door I turned and walked away slowly, convinced that the police would be on my tail.

Shit, what a mess I had got myself into.

I drove home and this time I was the one crying. Not much, but I was crying because I was scared of the repercussions. The Scotsman had my email and my telephone number and I'm sure a decent policeman would be able to find and charge me with GBH. Just then the phone rang. It was him. At first I didn't want to answer but eventually I did.

"Hello."

"Mistress."

"Yes, it's me. How are you?" I asked. "How's your foot? I'm sorry; I didn't mean to stamp down that hard."

"Don't you be worrying your pretty little head," he announced in a Glaswegian accent. "It was my fault. I asked you to do it."

Relief, he wasn't calling the police!

"So how are you?"

"I've never felt better and I've something to tell you."

"What, what is it?" I asked.

He told me that he'd come in his pants as he lay on the pavement and climaxed again as they attended to his foot in the Pharmacy. He'd refused to go to a hospital as he told them he had a plane to catch but suspected that he had broken something as he felt quite nauseous. They'd cleaned and strapped up his foot heavily and he couldn't get his shoe on but he bought some crutches and managed to limp to the taxi queue. He was doped up with pain killers he said, but he'd had quite a wonderful day, one of the best he could ever remember and of course he wanted to see me again for more of the same.

At first I thought of blocking him because I couldn't get my head around the stamping. This was the first time a client had asked me to physically assault them and it didn't sit comfortably with me. All sorts of scenarios flew around my brain. Was this just the start I thought? Would he jack up the violence to a new level if I agreed to go out with him again? And of course he'd frightened me when he'd grabbed me. I'd sleep on it I told myself. I reckoned I could cope with him and just needed to be more forceful, after all it had been one hell of a pay day.

I was still in a state of shock when I got home but poured myself a large glass of wine and counted up my day's earnings. I had over two hundred in cash as well as lingerie, perfume, clothes and some sex toys to the value of over nine hundred pounds. It hadn't been a bad day I suppose and if he really wanted to see me again I could always raise my fee.

I reached for my private phone and studied the picture of Edward I had taken the previous week. He had a small bath towel wrapped around him, my God he was gorgeous! I pushed the image of the Scotsman into the far reaches of my mind and tried to concentrate on Edward's beautiful form.

And it worked. Half way through the glass of wine the Scotsman was a distant memory and I focused on what I was going to do with my beautiful man when I surprised him in about four hours time.

Chapter Twelve

I had texted Edward asking when we were next seeing each other but hadn't had any reply. I wasn't too worried as he had mentioned something about a big meeting which I was sure was happening today. I would do everything in my power to relax my man with a fantastic evening he would never forget. As I got closer to his apartment I could feel myself getting more aroused thinking about the first night he had taken me against the window with the city lights twinkling below us, then the piano. My God, it was turning me on like I had never believed possible.

I pulled into the underground car park and switched off the engine and checked myself in the mirror. I positioned my stockings and garter belt through the thin material of my dress, a dress I didn't intend to have on very long and buttoned up my Burberry mac as I climbed out of the car. My stilettos I had been stamping on piggy's foot with just a few hours prior made a loud but determined clicking noise as I walked across to where the lifts were.

In the lift I reapplied my lippy and eyeliner, opened a bottle of Chanel and gave myself a little freshen up. I confess I was raring to go and feeling like a million dollars.

As I used the key fob Edward had given to me to activate the lift my whole body was quivering with anticipation and my pussy was doing cartwheels by the time the lift doors opened. But this was a different feeling, one I don't think I had ever experienced because although I was hot and eager for sex there was also the feeling that I just wanted to hold him and kiss him and be there with him. The man was taking over my life and I loved every second of it.

The anticipation was building as I tiptoed down the corridor towards his door. If he wasn't in there was a key he hid in a plant pot by his door so I had a plan B and would wait for him coming home. I'd climb into bed naked and give him the surprise of his life.

As it happened I didn't need the key because I tried the handle and ah ha it was open which meant he was in there somewhere. I pushed the door open a few inches and untied my mac, slipping it off my shoulders, I hung it quietly on the coat stand by the door and walked on in.

"Oh Edward," I called out quietly.

Nothing.

"Edward?"

I waited half a minute, still nothing. Perhaps he forgot to lock the door this morning?

I walked across the open sitting room looking for signs that he might be in, a warm coffee cup or a television playing somewhere but there was nothing. Then I heard a noise, it came from the bedroom. Was the TV in there switched on, had he come in from work and lay down on the bed and fallen asleep? I crept quietly towards the bedroom then I heard it, the unmistakable sound of a moan, Edward's moan. My heart pounded as I picked up my pace. I felt sick, my mind was a whirling mess as I suddenly realised why he hadn't called or even answered his bloody phone.

I reached the door and my hand hovered over the handle I didn't want to touch because I knew at that precise moment what I would find when I pushed the door open. But then no. My brain switched into a different mode of thinking as I clutched at straws. He was watching porn perhaps, the moaning was coming from the TV? A louder moan this time and now I knew that they weren't coming from the TV because those moans were more than familiar. I bit my lip and pushed down on the door handle and gave the door a push.

It was my worst possible nightmare. I wanted to scream, I wanted to cry as Edward lay on the bed with his eyes closed in ecstasy as a blond girl on all fours knelt over him servicing his cock for all she was worth.

I did scream. It was involuntary as I just wanted to turn and run but Edward's eyes flashed open at the sound and the realisation that he'd been caught registered in his face. I wanted to shout and swear at the two of them but the words wouldn't come. But the tears were coming and my eyes welled up as I stood frozen in shock as my entire world caved in. Edward almost kicked the girl four feet into the air as he clambered for his robe lying on the floor.

I just stared; I could feel my whole body go cold and the goose bumps standing up on my skin. I was angry, hurt, disappointed and I didn't know what to say or how to react.

Eventually I found a few words.

"Oh please, don't stop on my account Edward. It rather seemed as though you were enjoying that, is she good?"

I almost felt a twinge of sympathy for the poor girl as she crawled and hid around the side of the bed. After all, she probably didn't even know about me. How many other women did Edward have performing sexual favours for him?

I thought about all the lovely things he had done for me and the special things he'd said to me and wondered if they were the same lines he fed to the rest of them.

He had pulled on his robe in record time. I wanted out of there now! I turned to go.

"Please wait," he said. "It's not what you think."

It had to be the stupidest line he had ever uttered.

"It's not what I think?" I said, as I stood with my hands on my hips. "She was sucking your cock Edward; tell me Edward, what should I be thinking?"

I was already turning on my Jimmy's and strutting across what now seemed like a ridiculously large apartment as this pathetic excuse for a man stammered his excuses and apologies. I kept walking and on reflection didn't hear a word he was saying as I reached the door and almost ran towards the elevator, pressing the button and praying to God the lift was still there.

No such luck. Fuck, fuck, fuck, I just wanted out of there as I turned slowly and tried to look casual leaning against the wall as I waited for the lift. Despite the calm exterior, inside I was dying.

Edward stood a few yards from me as the elevator pinged.

I reached into my pocket for the key fob to the lift.

"These are yours; I won't be needing them anymore."

I tossed the key fob at his feet.

"Say something please!" he yelled as I stepped into the lift. "Please wait Jess, I can explain."

"I don't think so Edward," I spat, as the lift door closed on him and that was it.

I buttoned up my coat and the floodgates opened as I cried like a baby. My legs gave way and I sank into the corner of the lift in a heap.

In the car park I turned off my phone as I knew the calls and texts would start to flood in.

I was devastated; there was no other word to describe it and for the first forty eight hours I spent my time in bed with the duvet pulled over me, crying or drinking tea. Tea was the only thing I could keep down, even a coffee was somehow too strong a flavour to swallow and food was completely out of the question. Why had he done this to me? Everything had been so good, he was perfect and the sex was amazing. He was everything I'd ever dreamed. My head was in a complete mess and I drifted between wanting to physically hurt him in an act of violent revenge to thinking I had done something wrong and didn't deserve him.

It took me a few days to get my head right but eventually I came to the conclusion that surely I had been the perfect lover. I took care of my appearance, dressed nicely and as I've said the sex was more than fine and I had never once failed to pleasure him when I had been asked to. Women have a slight advantage during a sexual encounter in that we know for sure when the man has been satisfied, the male orgasm is impossible to fake. I had satisfied Edward again and again, I hadn't been overbearing or pushy and all of our dates had been suggested or planned by him. No, he'd no reason to take on another lover, no other reason than he was being greedy and deceiving me. I couldn't bear the thought of him with another woman and that's why I'd placed myself firmly out of the equation.

After two days I'd confined Edward to history and although it was hard I made my mind up that I had to get on with life. I'd shed many tears and they were all for him but I'd cried enough. I told myself that the tears would water the seeds of my future happiness.

I switched my phone back on; it was the first part of the healing process. There were twenty five missed calls, a dozen from him and the same number of text messages. I didn't listen to any of his messages nor did I read his texts. Fuck him; he didn't even have the balls to come round to my house. I blocked Edward's number there and then, made myself some cheese on toast and forced a cup of coffee down my throat. It was hard but I just about kept everything down and was rewarded thirty minutes later with a rush of energy.

Poor Russell, he hadn't had a walk and must have been sick of the sight of the back garden. I'd make up for it.

"Sorry Russ," I said, as I picked him up and gave him a cuddle.

I remember reading somewhere that cuddling a dog was as soothing to the mind and heart as deep meditation and almost as good for the soul as prayer. Russell felt wonderful as his little tail wagged and I said the magic word.

"Walkies."

So that's what we did... for hours. I walked Russell until his little legs nearly dropped off. I walked him through forests and up hills and one day I even drove to a beach so that he could feel the sand beneath his paws. It was great, just the therapy I needed even though one day the heavens opened and it rained cats and dogs. I loved every glorious minute of it. I told myself Edward wasn't worth it and this little Jack Russell was all I needed to get my life back on track. Little Russell loved me, little Russell was the most faithful companion I could ever wish for and he loved me more than he loved himself and that was special.

I spent a lot of time reading and cooking at home whilst I gathered my thoughts. And one day as I walked past a travel agents looking at all those nice warm places my body ached for the sun. I went in and collected a few magazines. California looked tempting and well within my budget but then I spotted a special deal that would take me to the Indian Ocean and the white sands of Mauritius. 'I'll think about it' I thought as I headed home.

Russell greeted me at the front door and I knew I couldn't desert him. He had comforted me through the whole Edward thing and I was going to reward him with two weeks in kennels, which he hated. Some sort of heartless bitch I was. There was only one solution to get through this and that was to immerse myself in my work. I'd give it a month or two and I'd book a five star hotel in Scotland, one with a pool and a spa and a nice restaurant and a bar, but I'd only book one that would allow Russell to come along too.

The brochures for Mauritius and California went straight in the bin and I switched on the computer for the first time in ten days. I searched a few hotels in Edinburgh and Aberdeenshire and somewhere called the Trossachs and then my mouth fell open as the search engine took me to Gleneagles, a luxury five star hotel in its own grounds in Perthshire. Perfect for Russell and although it was quite expensive I figured that a couple of decent real time clients would cover the cost. I bookmarked the page and then clicked onto my Mistress Zeta email box.

Seventy seven mails. Oh my God! Someone did love me after all I thought. I began to filter them out, at least fifty per cent of them a complete waste of time and another ten asking me to do things that I just wouldn't contemplate. But this one I was reading now bordered on the ridiculous. I swear this man was living on another planet, mentally deranged or both, but these sorts of requests were becoming more and more commonplace as my client circle grew ever wider.

'Hi.

I wondered if you would do a short custom video for me. The outfit would be a sexy bra and a mini skirt and a thong, also sexy high heels. The theme is giantess, so you will need some tiny men (really small scale, less than one inch).'

What the bloody hell was this man on? I will need some tiny men? Oh that's easy enough; I think Tesco covers that range. I read on.

'It has been only a few days since you stole the growth formula and grew hundreds of feet tall, but you are

132

already used to being a giantess, actually, you consider yourself as a goddess, THE Goddess.

You appear suddenly, walking confidently with a bunch of tiny men (same scale as always) in your hand. On your way to the bed you find some tiny men on the floor and you call them: "Insignificant human insects" and crush them. Then as you are about to sit down on the bed you discover there are a group of tiny men near you. You just sit on them and smile. Then start to eat them, saying that if you want to be bigger and more powerful you need to eat those insects in your hand. You do this in a sexy manner, licking your fingers, dropping them into your wide open mouth or licking them from your palm. While you eat you rub your boobs and pussy, dropping some of them in your panties and bra ordering them to masturbate the Goddess. You describe how easy it was to destroy the last city you visited and the huge amount of people you ate, fucked and crunched. This turns you on greatly.'

Did this man think I was some sort of movie maker with access to err.. inch high men? Or was he lost in his own little fantasy and forgetting that I was a human being, an online dominatrix? At this point I wanted to close down the computer and reach for a bottle of gin, but I felt compelled to read on. Surely he would get to the point soon and tell me that it was all fantasy. Perhaps he would want me to pretend he was an inch high? I didn't know where he was going on this; surely the punch line was coming soon?

'Then you finish the last one and realise that you must have been growing a lot in the last few days, because you are not full yet. This must result in you moving on to bigger cities where you can find lots of humans to eat and play with. Describe in detail what you did to the last cities, like destroying buildings, crushing cars and killing thousands of people, like The Goddess of the Humans that you are.

By this point you now have more humans in a jar so as you may eat them on your way to the next city and also you can use them to pleasure yourself, putting them everywhere in your body, and masturbating till you come. When you are finished you smile, put your panties on again (not the bra) and go for another city to conquer calling yourself The Goddess of the World and saying that you cannot wait until you grow big enough to eat the whole planet.

Whilst walking away you find another tiny man. You are about to crush him but then change your mind and pick him up. You tell him that he is very lucky because you are willing to keep him as a personal pet on your way to conquer the world. Then you put him in your panties. This last part should be like around two to three minutes. Then you leave the place.

'During the whole clip you have to act like you LOVE to be the Goddess of the World, you are really evil and do such terrible things.'

My jaw was at the level of the computer desk, seven hundred words of utter shit. I replied to him, much against my better judgement but I replied. I told him to put the inch high men in his pants and they could wank him off and save the two of us a whole lot of time and effort.

I then blocked his email address. I hope he got the message.

The next one was another request for a lunch humiliation. I'd done a few of these in the past and they paid well and were relatively harmless.

'Dear Mistress,

I have been trying to summon the courage to book a humiliation lunch or dinner session with you and I feel I may be finally ready. I have been fantasising about being seen in public with you whilst you torment and humiliate me. I would love to have lunch with you and sit there whilst you degrade and embarrass me in front of the waiter. I was thinking that I could pay you the full amount upfront so that it would prevent me from backing out from making this fantasy into a reality.

I really hope that we can arrange a date for this week sometime; I will work around you my dear Mistress.

Thank you in advance
Lunch Loser.'

This was a nice one to 'ease' back into it I thought as I read through it again. I replied saying that I could do the weekend but I was to be paid the fee of five hundred pounds upfront. Within a few minutes whilst wading through the other emails he replied agreeing and promising to deposit the money into my account within the hour. We agreed a time and my outfit and I finished the rest of my emails.

Chapter Thirteen

The domination session couldn't come quick enough for me and it was exactly what I needed. I had chosen a restaurant out of town because I certainly didn't ever want to go back there and be recognised. I took Russell with me. I had a cunning plan as I pulled into the hotel car park and Russell settled down on his blanket on the front seat. I patted him on the head and told him I wouldn't be long. This man wanted me to cause a scene and that was exactly what he was going to get.

It was a Hilton Hotel and we met outside as arranged. A man pushing fifty, short, with the type of hair that they call a comb-over approached me and introduced himself as Reg. He was clearly bald but was fighting against it with determination to be admired, he had more hairspray than I did as a gentle breeze blew across the car park and his hair never moved a millimetre.

I walked forcefully into reception and stood at the counter as the receptionist looked on.

"I want a room for tonight," I demanded.

He looked a little surprised and stepped forward.

"One single room," I said loudly. "You can wipe that smile from your face."

And he did. And he took his credit card out and paid for the best room in the place, not a single room as it happened but a suite he would never see, a suite that would suit me and Russell just fine.

I played the bitch well and ordered a bottle of champagne to be delivered to the room at midnight.

"One glass will suffice," I announced, scowling at him as he cringed and took out his credit card once again and settled the transaction.

We made our way to the restaurant at the far end of reception and he casually whispered that I was playing the part exactly as he'd hoped for. I followed his email instruction to the letter as the maître d' welcomed us and showed us to the pre-booked table. I was on my client's case immediately complaining about everything and anything he contemplated ordering. Between me, him and the waiter and the ten minute decision making process I don't think he had a clue what he was going to eat.

But we waited, and as the first course arrived I rounded on him. He'd ordered foie gras and I raised my voice as he put the first forkful into his mouth. I berated him about the savage cruelty of the dish he was savouring while he protested he'd never wanted it in the first place.

I was doing a good job as people started to take notice and turn around. The waiter intervened; he said there wasn't a problem if he wanted to change. I ordered him to eat every last forkful and hoped he would choke on it. He looked genuinely uncomfortable as he cleared every last bit from his plate.

He had ordered fish for the main course but before it arrived I called the waiter over.

"He's changed his mind," I said." He wants a fillet steak, medium rare."

He offered a token resistance.

"Err no darling, I'd rather have the fish."

I gently placed my fork on the plate.

"You'll have the steak you selfish pig, aren't you forgetting about Russell? He hasn't eaten since breakfast time."

The waiter and my dining partner looked on in confusion.

I leaned forward and glared.

"The dog you idiot, he's in the car and he'll be starving."

Reg didn't know where to look but the penny finally dropped as he turned to the waiter and agreed the change.

"I'll have it well done," he said.

"Medium rare," I snapped.

He looked at the waiter and nodded in agreement.

When the huge piece of fillet steak arrived I leaned over, picked up his steak knife and sawed it in half.

"The big bit is for Russell is that clear?"

"Yes dear."

I picked fault with him the whole night and refused to allow him a drop of alcohol while I sampled the finest champagne, knowing I had a bed for the night. Reg begged me for a glass of wine but I flatly refused. I timed my best insults as the waiter or the maître d' approached the table quietly making a point of ridiculing his performance in bed and the size of his tiny cock.

As the effect of the alcohol kicked in I even started to enjoy myself and had to concentrate really hard on insulting Reg. The thing is, he was actually very nice and some of the things I said to him got to me and I had to remind myself that it was all part of the act. When the final bill game Reg placed his credit card on the silver plate and when the transaction was complete Reg placed a five pound note down on the table by way of a tip. As the waiter thanked him and picked up the note I rounded on Reg calling him the tightest twat under the sun and I wasn't going to be placated until he had put a twenty pound note down on the table.

And so the session was over and I stormed through reception in a strop while Reg ran after me. I picked up my room key in reception and in full view and earshot of everyone in the vicinity I told Reg to fuck off and die and that I never wanted to see him again. I then remembered what Reg had detailed in his email so I took a deep breath for courage and slapped him hard across his face.

"Oh my God thank you so much Mistress," he groaned, his face red from the firm slap I had just planted on him.

"That was an amazing experience," he gushed. "I really must dash."

He winked at me as he said that last bit and I knew he was going to go and find the nearest rest room so he could jack off.

That was his cue to scurry away and a minute or two later I went out into the car park to collect Russell. As always he greeted me as if I was the last person on earth and we made our way through reception to the lifts. The suite was beautiful and the champagne was waiting for me.

I reached into my bag and pulled out the piece of fillet steak I'd wrapped in a serviette during dinner.

We curled up together in a king size bed with our bellies full and slept like babies. I had earned five hundred quid and we'd both had a feast fit for a king. Surely there were worse jobs in the world?

When I arrived home the next day I switched on my computer and opened my first mail of the day. Suddenly I'd lost that feel-good factor and my stomach was in knots. The email almost wanted me to retch as I realised the sort of men I was dealing with. Thankfully they were in the cyberspace world and they could easily be deleted and blocked. But the content of this pervert's email stayed with me for several days and it concerned me that he was writing as if he clearly knew me. It also made me almost physically sick that he had apparently found several girls who were willing to act out his warped fantasy.

'Dear Mistress,

I wrote to you some time ago asking for a real time meeting but you said at the time you were not doing them. I asked about shopping humiliation however, and you replied that you would consider it.

To be honest, while shopping would be nice I have another fantasy I would like to discuss with you and pray that you will consider it. You definitely are amazing and have redefined my ultimate dominant woman as I didn't think someone as beautiful as you even existed.

I want to be your human toilet to show you how wonderful you are by drinking your piss for a day as your toilet slave. This isn't weird. It's clean and will be clear pee only and sterile and just shows my ultimate gift of submission. I have done this for several other girls and they like using my mouth for the day and its a win win situation as I am very quiet, pay well and they only see me when they use my body to consume their waste. We can go to a hotel if you like and you can lock me in the bathroom until you need to piss and then use my mouth. You can get on with whatever you want, watch TV, read a book or whatever.

I enjoy it and the girls tell me they feel very powerful.

Please Goddess, please let me be your nice gentle toilet slave and use my mouth to pee into. Just water sports only! Please, please allow me to be your toilet. Please let me know as I think you're so beautiful and sexy and my favourite woman in the whole world.'

The two nicest words on a computer, delete – block.

Chapter Fourteen

I was now working more than fifty hours a week and the money was rolling in. I was turning away clients by the boatload, some because they were depraved, others because I just didn't have the time. For the first time I was being selective, cherry picking if you like and the more I worked, the less time I had to think about the betrayal.

The main site I worked for had sent me a link to set up a 'domme' line to my mobile phone. This was a little different and to be perfectly frank sounded like money for old rope. I read the terms and conditions and that none of the callers would be able to see my number and I could decline the calls if it wasn't convenient. I could also set up a schedule where I would appear online or offline and could set the rate that I wanted. I decided pretty quickly that I had nothing to lose and it would be another outlet for earning decent money if I could pitch the rate right. I set my rate at five pounds a minute. It was expensive I know and I thought I wouldn't have too many takers at that sort of price but if nothing happened it was an easy enough matter to come down in price and reset it.

I registered the account and clicked activate. It was six o'clock in the evening and I figured I'd give it a few days and if nothing happened I'd try a new rate. What I didn't realise was that now I'd activated the account I was effectively 'live' and if I didn't feel like taking calls I should have set my setting to 'offline.' So, at around eleven later that night as I lay in bed watching TV sipping a glass of red my phone started ringing with a long strange number displayed as the caller ID. and realised I had my first caller.

"Shit!"

I didn't want a caller, I was tucked up in bed and feeling a little tired until I remembered I was on five pounds a minute.

"Yes," I answered in a husky drawl.

"Mistress?" said a desperate little voice.

"Yes this is she, what do you want? What is your fantasy?"

I guessed that would be a good start, finding out what they wanted. He'd caught me totally unaware and I was a little nervous as this was my first time and didn't expect a call just hours after signing up. Bizarrely my mind flashed back to one of those American films where the police have a kidnapper on the line and they try to keep them talking for as long as possible so they can trace the call. And here I was; I was that policeman.

He spoke again breaking me from my thoughts.

"I errr I want you to call me names and tell me I have a small dick."

I shook my head, Christ, and I started to giggle for real.

"And yes Mistress I want you to laugh at me."

I waited a while as I laughed a little louder.

"Oh my God loser you are one sad bastard you really are."

I looked at my watch; the first minute had passed... five quid. Keep him talking.

"You have such a small dick it's pathetic. Look at it? It's like a cocktail sausage."

"Yes Mistress it is, I'm so useless. I couldn't possibly hope to please a woman like you."

"God no, not ever, that cock is pitiful, isn't it, pencil dick?"

I was laughing hard now as I realised how surreal this was, it was harmless, but it was still a different world. This bloke was getting off on being told he had a small cock! You couldn't make that up! I kept him talking, I could hear him breathing heavy and I heard the sound of clothing rustling and I figured his member was now in his sweaty little hands.

"Yes Mistress, it's like a crayon, it's tiny and thin, oh God I'm a loser."

He panted and whined and his breathing sounded laboured.

"You're playing with yourself aren't you pencil dick?"

"Yes Mistress."

"Are you wanking hard? You really are a tiny cock loser, a loser with a small willy trying to get off." I laughed.

"I love it when you laugh at me Mistress."

He was panting loudly now and loving every second.

I tried to keep him talking but the more I insulted him the more I could hear him getting ever closer to where it was he wanted to be. Towards the end of the call it was me who did all the talking, he was incapable.

"That's it loser, beat it harder, wank for your Mistress pin dick."

"Yes Mistress."

And then he came. He screamed out loud and he relieved himself and now I couldn't laugh as I pictured the mess he'd produced all over his trousers or wherever.

"You dirty bastard, you've climaxed haven't you and without my permission."

"Yes Mistress, I'm sorry Mistress it won't happen again."

I needed to keep him talking and yet what do you say to a man who has just jacked off?

"Where have you come loser, in your trousers you filthy bastard?"

"On a paper tissue Mistress."

I cringed, I wanted to throw the phone over to the other side of the room. I was beginning to feel unclean, as if it had been my hand pleasuring the pathetic creature. I kept him talking for another four minutes talking about his paper tissues and of course his tiny willy. I told him to go and clean up and I would be waiting for him. He agreed.

"Give me a minute Mistress, I'll be back soon and we can arrange our next session, I've enjoyed myself so much."

What a stroke of genius. The dirty bastard was away for nearly three minutes cleaning up and I turned the TV up a little and watched the Sky News headlines. And then he was back.

"I'm back Mistress."

I was growing weary and struggling to come up with things to say and didn't want to push my luck. If this bloke thought I was taking the mickey then perhaps he wouldn't call back. So I abused him some more and told him to fuck off and towards the end of the call he begged me to let him call again.

"I'll think about it." I said

And while he started to whine on again I pressed 'end call'.

I'd ended the call so he couldn't possibly think that I'd dragged the conversation out. I checked my watch. Thirteen minutes, sixty five pounds for lying in bed having a laugh. I'd had worse jobs. I chuckled to myself wondering what I had signed up for.

My phone line business picked up. I got two calls a few days later and the next after that I got three. The phone wasn't exactly red hot but by the end of the month I was averaging a hundred pounds a day. Now I know that's not mega money by any stretch of the imagination but that's twenty minutes on the phone, that's all. I would take calls whenever possible which meant sometimes slipping off to the restroom whilst lunching with the girls or finding a quiet aisle while doing the grocery shopping. It was really quite entertaining if I'm honest but sometimes a bit embarrassing. I remember being in Sainsbury's one day when I took a call. I made sure I slipped into a quiet aisle as the fun and games built up and the conversation grew more explicit.

The caller wanted me to pretend we were husband and wife and play out that he had caught me having an affair. This was the phone call where he would ask me what I saw in my new boyfriend, what he had that my pretend husband didn't and of course it came down to cock size again. (Surprise, surprise.)

Picture the scene.

"I'm sorry Tom, I didn't mean to hurt you but I have to be honest with you."

I was in full flow.

"His cock is the biggest I've ever seen and compared to your pathetic tiny member you just don't satisfy me anymore. I love cock Tom, I love big cocks and therefore you're history and I want a divorce."

I was getting carried away and hadn't spotted the dear old lady reaching for a jar of jam.

"You're cock doesn't satisfy me anymore don't you get it? I like them big and I like them hard."

I heard the crash and the aisle was awash with blackcurrant jam with an old lady on the verge of a heart attack as she steadied herself on the cereal shelf. My God, I was out of that supermarket as quick as lightning and switched to Tesco for my weekly shop soon afterwards, at least for a few months anyway. I would simply die if I came into contact with that poor lady again.

I took the phone calls wherever I could and if I say so myself polished my art to perfection. Fifteen minutes, seventy five pounds was my target and I achieved precisely that with most of the calls although some of the callers were determined to finish themselves off in under five minutes. When that happened I roasted them and told them not to call back if they couldn't stay the distance. I took more calls in the supermarkets or on shopping trips to town, I took them in the toilets of bars and restaurants, in the petrol stations and in the street and I took them from dawn until midnight but only when it was convenient to me.

One man rang me nearly every day. He was on the phone for nearly ten minutes, fifty pounds a day!

I play the make-believe girlfriend of this little dreamer. I degrade him by letting him know that I have sex with other men and I describe every explicit detail as I hear him whimper on the other end of the phone. I tell him what underwear I wear for the dates and describe the dresses and shoes for nights out where I will try to pick up other guys. He tells me he is married in real life and likes to think that his wife is carrying on with other men like this but of course can't pick up the courage to confront her. Most of the phone calls end in tears, his tears, when he begs me to stop playing around and I tell him to go and jack himself off because he won't be getting any action from me.

I'm amazed, even today, at how many variations this particular fetish comes in. It appears that every month this industry throws up another surprise; no one could ever describe it as a dull occupation. It had been a pretty intense month with a more than satisfactory level of earnings from the domme line, half a dozen real time sessions and more than twenty Skype sessions from around the globe. My earnings for the month had been the best ever, sixteen thousand pounds and yet I'd still managed a few nights out with the girls, a shopping trip to London, dinner at my mothers and the weekend at Gleneagles with Russell.

Now that was something special. Even the drive up to Scotland was pleasant and relaxing, at least after I had left the motorway near Carlisle that is. I took the A74 through Lockerbie and Moffat, as I headed towards the Kincardine Bridge that took me over the River Forth. The last hour and a half driving towards Auchterarder was so spectacular, surely some of the best scenery I have seen anywhere in the world. It was late afternoon by the time we arrived and I walked Russell around the grounds by the golf courses before getting changed and enjoying a wonderful dinner in one of the bars. It was pricey to stay at Gleneagles, of course it was, but I was enjoying the good life and it was made all the more special knowing that I had paid for it from my own hard earned cash. It wasn't the easiest business to be in but if you were mentally strong enough and worked it correctly the rewards were more than satisfactory.

Life was good and I was slowly but surely getting over the heartache of Edward's betrayal, in fact to be quite honest he hardly figured in my thoughts. I was streamlining the business and getting rid of the timewasters and anyone who made me want to vomit. And believe me there were plenty of those. Most of the new requests coming in to my email box would get binned as my client base was almost where I wanted it to be. However there was always an odd new case that would interest me and if they did I would quote a ridiculously high price and wait for them to bite. Eighty per cent I would never hear from again but the remaining twenty per cent would have the funds deposited within the hour and we'd be in business. As more high earners came in I would drop the low paid jobs and build up the net worth of each job accordingly.

Sat at the laptop one day I opened an email. He started by telling me he was head of an IT firm and he would like to talk to me about his fantasy. I emailed him back and asked him to tell me what it was he was looking for.

He replied quickly stating that he wished to be blackmailed by me, I was to use pictures that he would send me.

Confused, I wrote back to clarify his wishes and he repeated that I would order him to do various embarrassing things then he would set the automatic timer on his camera, take pictures and send them to me. I'd get him to do these things by acting in a very seductive yet dominating way, wrapping him around my finger and then telling him that seeing the photos of him doing naughty things really turned me on.

I would then call him up and proceed to blackmail him, threatening to post the pictures on the internet or send them to his place of work. He wrote that I could blackmail him for gifts and money and he said that if it was mutually rewarding he would like to act out the fantasy at least once a week. I wrote back setting my 'blackmail fee' at a thousand pounds. He replied instantly and emphasised that he wanted me to be a seductress in stage one of the plan and a complete bitch on stage two. That wasn't a problem, I replied, 'when can we begin'?

We played it rather low key at first, the first time he Skyped me I said I liked men who dressed up in stockings and suspenders, I said it made me hot. He didn't look at all surprised and then he started his act saying I'd never get him to do anything like that. I asked if he had any in the house. He said yes, his wife kept that sort of thing in her wardrobe.

"Please get them for me John, it turns me on so much, please baby, please do it for me."

And then he was out of the door and five minutes later he is back in front of the screen stripping himself naked and pulling on a pair of his wife's tiny knickers. Stockings next, then the frilly red suspenders and then unless I was very much mistaken the front of his tiny knickers was beginning to change shape. John, the head of one of London's top legal firms was developing a hard on.

By the time I persuaded him to get his camera, his cock was poking out the top of the knickers and the photograph was simply priceless as it came through on Skype. As instructed I ended the call and printed the screen shots off. I would call him in a few days when he was least expecting it, and it had to be when he was at work.

John told me he loved the feeling of being powerless, exploited and spoken to like dirt. At work he controls the show, there's no doubt about it and during his fantasy he isn't the big cheese anymore and that's what turns him on.

I called him back at ten in the morning on a Friday. He had given me a schedule of his working day and I knew he had an end of week meeting at this time.

"Hi darling," he answered. "It's not really convenient at the moment can you call me back?"

"Oh it's convenient John," I replied. "You'd better make it convenient because I have a photograph that I'm looking at right now that your dear colleagues would just love to see."

I heard John turn to whoever was in the room. He said that his girlfriend was on the phone and something urgent had cropped up. He finished the meeting abruptly. I heard them leave and he closed the door after them and then he was back. I told him to switch on his laptop and that I would be Skyping him within the minute. He did exactly as he was told.

John looked the picture of worry as he appeared in the middle of my Skype page. I held up the photograph and moved it a little closer to the camera as it focused into view.

"Look at this John, isn't it pretty?"

"Please darling no, please don't -"

"I think I'll be making a trip to the Post Office later on," I said. "It's just a shame I won't be there to see your secretary's face when she opens this. I'm sure that by lunchtime tomorrow everyone in the place will know what their beloved boss gets up to behind closed doors."

"Please darling no, don't send that. I'll do anything you want but please tear it up now."

It was music to my ears, John would do anything I wanted and so I demanded and got a thousand pounds credited to my bank account by the close of business. John sent me an email later that night to say that I had acted out his fantasy perfectly. I emailed a photograph of the ripped up photograph as agreed and then we started all over again.

Over time I notched up the humiliation level to maximum and John did anything I asked of him. One day he took a photograph of himself sucking on a dildo and inevitably I had pictures of him wanking and even a five minute video of him watching porn. But in general it was mostly dressing up in women's clothes but with wigs and makeup too. My God, surely his wife must be aware that he was using her things? But then I began to think. Did he even have a wife but if he did was she in on the act? I don't know and I never asked if there was a Mrs Moss. I think it's all very sad that the two of them didn't communicate and it could have been her acting out his harmless fantasy and saving a small fortune every month.

John is still one of my regular clients and he's actually a very nice man who I've grown to respect. He always sends me an email to thank me after each session and who am I to judge what turns people on? At least he is doing something about it and getting off and not hiding away and suffering in silence and misery like many men with similar tastes.

I feel very much like a therapist, that's the easiest way to describe my profession, and that's what it is, a profession. I also get men who are new to this type of fantasy play and who are still finding their feet so to speak. We work together and find out what they are comfortable with. I help them find that comfortable place by asking questions. Some like me to be seductive, others bitchy and some like me to be a full on dominatrix. So we test the water, sometimes for up to a month before we find a comfortable medium that they enjoy.

I had been working with one guy for about three weeks when I ordered him to do something and he made an oink sound like a pig. I thought perhaps it had been a bit of interference on the phone but then he did it for a second time.

"What the fuck are you doing loser?" I asked.

"I don't know Mistress," he said. "It just kind of came out."

The conversation continued, more oinks. He then told me he was doing it to remember he was inferior, that was fine by me, it takes all sorts as they say.

The oinker was another regular on my domme line, not quite every day of the week but at least twice. He'd ring me and greet me with an oink.

"Not you again Piggy," I'd say.

"Oink."

"You filthy, dirty swine."

"Oink."

And so the conversation continued until he built himself up to a level where he needed to relieve himself... about twelve minutes I think for the oinker. It was all in a day's work.

Chapter Fifteen

So life wasn't all that bad. My business was at a level I felt I could handle without it screwing my head up too badly. Believe me it can mess your head up. It's a profession where you have to know how to switch off. I told myself after every job that I was an actress and as I walked away I told myself that the cameras had shut down and I'd walked off the set after the director called cut!

I was now experienced at spotting the timewasters or the real perverts and they were blocked every time and even if they came through under a different email I learned to spot the signs in the first paragraph of any correspondence.

My earnings were good; over one hundred thousand a year to what amounted to about a twenty hour week and because I took an occasional client on most months, the earnings were heading in the right direction.

I worked smart; I worked on an hourly rate in excess of one hundred pounds and if my clients weren't willing to pay it they went the journey. It was about building that rate up and I worked on a business plan so that by the end of the year that rate would be around one hundred and fifty pounds. I had no shortage of clients and potential new clients; emails were coming in at the rate of about twenty a day as word went round the chat rooms and blogs of this particular fetish that Mistress Zeta was very good at her job. And I was, because whilst I pandered to their whims I also showed compassion and understood their needs exactly. Every single one of my clients were treated with the greatest respect and sympathy and yet I was also a bloody good actress so the role play or the fantasy we played out felt real to them. One thing never ceased to amaze me and that was the amount of money some of my clients spent on a regular basis. Not all of them were rich, some of them were ordinary working men, but spending in excess of a thousand pounds most months did not seem to faze them. I tried not to ask any personal questions about my clients lives but inevitably it happened occasionally. Some of them were only too pleased to boast about their professions or their wealth and yes, I regularly got 'my wife doesn't understand me' routine.

I remember one client in particular, a postman from Mount Pleasant Sorting Office in London who would openly admit the ridiculous amount of hours overtime he would need to work each month in order to afford his regular real time sessions with me. He worked the nightshift at Mount Pleasant and was paid a salary that worked out at fifteen pounds per hour. I read about it one day in the Daily Telegraph as the postmen were preparing to go on strike. I couldn't quite believe how little these men were paid and poor Bob worked an extra twenty five hours a month in order to afford his days out with Mistress Zeta. I almost felt sorry for him but then his 'thank you' emails after each session assured me that he thought it was money well spent so who was I to argue?

There was no man in my life other than Russell but I felt I could live with that. Okay, the physical and sensual side of sex wasn't there, and there wasn't any love in my life but I was still young and I had no real desire to jump into a full on relationship again. Edward had hurt me more than I probably cared to admit and it was maybe the internal scarring from that fall out that prevented me from taking an odd casual acquaintance any further. I put love firmly on the back burner and decided to concentrate on business for the foreseeable future.

I was taking Skype sessions and domme line calls from all over the English speaking world which was fine with me because it allowed me to plan my diary accordingly. I had a large map on my bedroom/office wall which showed the time differences in various parts of the world and I used red marker pins to show exactly where my customers were calling from. For example if a client emailed from New York requesting a session I knew that New York was five hours behind us and therefore a nine or ten pm call suited me and the client just fine. Washington was on the same time zone and on the other side of the world, Sydney was ten hours ahead of GMT and Wellington twelve and therefore I took those sessions between nine in the morning and noon.

My Brit clients fell in between those hours and as more international mails flooded in my business grew accordingly. I think the Americans in particular loved the idea that they were talking to a British girl and many clients told me how sexy they thought my accent was! Who was I to argue?

I had a request for a Skype session from a businessman from Los Angeles. I knew LA was eight hours behind and checked my diary. I didn't give him any options I said that if he wanted a session it would be a week on Wednesday at eight pm British time which meant noon for him. He confirmed the time and I instructed a one hundred and fifty dollars payment upfront which was in my account within three hours. I emailed back to say we were in business.

He explained in the email that he was a French National but had lived over there for some time. He sent me a role play he wanted acted out, fantasising that we were in a cuckold relationship and that he was very wealthy and lived every day in charge of many employees yet I always wore the trousers in the relationship. He said that after a long day's work he came home to find me – his fiancé – getting all dolled up ready to go out. I then proceeded to tell him that I was going out on a date and if he wanted me to go through with our future wedding plans that he would have to accept this and turn a blind eye to my indiscretions. As he was older than me I had to act on the fact that he should be grateful a sexy young girl like me would even be interested in an old man like him!

When I saw François I guess I quite fancied him. He was a very nice looking man, immaculately groomed and very well put together, I guessed around forty years of age and strangely quite confident in front of the cameras which was more than a little unusual. Most of my clients are nervous, timid and take some time to relax but François was exactly the opposite.

The first session lasted thirty minutes and it was me who did most of the talking as François asked me to describe what I had been doing on my make believe date and what my young stud was like. It was all pretty straight forward really.

"Oh François you wouldn't believe the beautiful body he has, it's toned and muscular and suntanned, unlike yours and you can tell he works out in the gym. We went out for a little dinner at your favourite restaurant but he told me not to eat too much as I had some hard work ahead of me."

"And what did he mean by that?" François asked.

"Oh François you are a real cretin aren't you? What do you think he meant?"

I would then go on to describe my date, my ideal man, attentive and kind and yet an animal in between the sheets and of course he had the hugest cock you could imagine and stamina to match! I don't know why but men seem to be fascinated by other men's big willies! Don't ask me why but they are. I could tell François was getting turned on as I described how my 'date' had made me orgasm again and again and took care to belittle François' lovemaking and as always the size of his member. He asked more and more questions and the session ran over as he apologised and said he would make it up to me. He did. He dropped an extra two hundred dollars into my account with an email asking to set up weekly appointments. It was fine by me.

It was about two months into our regular sessions when François said something which made me laugh.

"I'd love you to come out here and live with me in LA and then you could be my full time Mistress."

"You and everyone else François; you couldn't afford me."

François laughed.

"I don't think money would be an issue."

I looked at my watch, the session was coming to an end and I had learnt very quickly that there were a lot of timewasters out there in cyberspace, A LOT! It was so mind-numbingly predictable what some customers would come out with.

"Time to go François, I have some more calls to do."

"I don't want you to do any more calls, I want you all to myself," he said.

Now that was a really strange thing to come from the mouth of a cuckold.

"I don't think so François."

But he was being persistent.

"What about a holiday then, I'll fly you over first class and you can take as long as you like to think about it."

"My business here is fine François," I said. "I make good money and I have no one to answer too except my little Jack Russell."

Shit! As soon as the words had tumbled from my mouth I knew I had slipped up. This was personal stuff, things the clients should never hear and not only had I told him there was no one in my life I'd even told him about Russell.

He was fishing now.

"So there's no one special," he said.

"Time's up," I said rather abruptly. "I have to get going, speak next week."

"I want more Zeta," he said.

"It's Mistress Zeta to you," I corrected sharply.

I was in a fluster and without another word I pressed end call. I was tired, that was it. I was tired and I'd slipped up and I made myself a promise that it wouldn't happen again. I lay in bed looking at the ceiling as my eyelids grew progressively heavier. Eventually I drifted off dreaming of a short break in LA.

My domme line was proving to be a substantial income but it seemed that François was not taking no for an answer when it came to my declining of the offer to be his fulltime 'Mistress girlfriend.' At first I didn't realise it was him calling the line as he had lived in the states for such a long time his native accent only broke through his perfected American twang during parts of his sentences. On the third consecutive day my new client called, I suspected it was him and I came right out with it.

"Good afternoon François."

I expected him to be stunned that I'd guessed it was him but he just started to laugh.

"Do you enjoy having to pay to speak to me?" I asked coolly whilst I finished applying my makeup. "This is a lot more expensive than a Skype call and you can't even see me."

"The money is irrelevant Zeta," he said, "I will do whatever it takes to get your attention and convince you that my offer was serious."

"I have told you before it's Mistress to you, remember that."

I was a little put out and more than confused. Why didn't he speak to me via Skype, why the deception?

I jumped in with both feet and regretted it instantly.

"I'd be only too happy to sit my little designer clad ass on a BA Business Class flight to LA at your expense but how would I know it wasn't Ted Bundy who'd collect me at the airport?" I retorted.

"Ted Bundy was executed in 1989 Zeta; he won't be at the airport."

He'd put me on the spot with a clever reply. François was not a nutcase, I knew that from our dozens of conversations, conversations that I'd started to look forward too.

"Look François I'm busy right now so you can book a Skype session for tonight if you want but I won't be coming to LA and nothing you say will make me change my mind."

Before he could form his next sentence I cut the call short and regretted it.

Shit! I had always wanted to go to LA and had never set foot on US soil, so was more than tempted at the prospect of considering a 'business trip'. And yet I knew it was crazy, things like that just didn't happen to Jessica Black and anyway I wouldn't be able to conduct my business if I was at his beck and call and therefore I would undoubtedly lose clients. Stupid, stupid, stupid!

I returned home and did a couple of Skype sessions and watched a film in bed with you guessed it Russell! As I lay watching 'The Devil Wears Prada" I couldn't help thinking about the offer François had made and yet I had worked my business to the point I was making great money for very little work. Of course I was still a little uncomfortable with the industry but knew I was mentally strong enough to cope. I knew there was something missing in my life but surely this wasn't my calling and there had to be something more?

I found myself thinking more and more of François and of course a trip to LA. I could leave my business for a week or two couldn't I?

Just then the laptop pinged on the floor next to the bed interrupting my thoughts. An email. It was François. I groaned as I opened it and waited for it to load. It was taking a fair while, photographs loading, big files; the text said they were pictures of his Malibu home.

Eventually they downloaded. Holy shit! This place was insane. It was gorgeous, a pool with roman pillars and gardens overlooking the beach below.

'This is waiting for you' was the subject of the email. I'll say one thing for François he was persistent! There were also more attachments, pictures of shoes and a dress he had purchased from one of my many wish lists the American site I was featured on insisted we have. He had spent three hundred dollars on a black tight satin dress and over a thousand on a pair of Christian Louboutin shoes. What the hell was it with these guys and bloody Louboutin shoes?! The purchases he'd made would have paid my monthly mortgage payments twice over. Well, at least I now knew he was probably sincere about paying for a trip to LA and yet I was convinced it wasn't going to happen. My fingers hovered over the key pad... I was still unsure. In a flash of inspiration I typed 'convince me' and then I switched the laptop off.

I spent a sleepless night thinking about the direction my life was going in and longed to live like they did on the film I had been watching. I wondered if the purchases François had made were perhaps just a little over the top. Don't get me wrong, I absolutely loved receiving gifts, I mean who doesn't but I hadn't even worked for those things, he'd just gone out and bought them and said they were waiting for me when I arrived in LA. The shopping trips with clients were different, they were payment for my services and my time and I didn't have a problem with them.

I tried to switch off and get some sleep to prepare myself for the few sessions I had the following day but I spent a restless night and woke up feeling like shit!

It was early when I decided to get up and I sat in the kitchen window looking out at the bright start to the day. The radio was on in the background and I hit start on the coffee machine as the Mac fired up and my day started. Two email requests for real time sessions caught my attention, one had been sent during the night so I guessed he was from America. I was right

'Hello Dear Mistress,

A friend of mine has recommended you to me, he says you really are the very best and we have chatted many times about the fantastic services you offer. I am to be In London this week and would love to make your acquaintance, possibly some lunch and a spot of shopping. I would love for you to flirt with the waiters and sales staff, make me feel you can do so much better than me. If you would accept my booking I would like you to play the role of my girlfriend and I can see by your profile that you are much younger than me, which is exactly what I want. I love the way you look.'

I looked at the time the email was sent once again, it looked like a US west coast time difference and the name of the email yourcuck@gmail.com started me thinking.

No, it couldn't possibly be you know who could it? I got up to fill my cup with fresh coffee. I sat back down and hit reply.

'Morning Cuck, and where are you travelling from? What day do you wish to book your appointment and how much are you willing to spend for my services?'

I pressed send, if I was correct and it was in fact a US customer I would not get a reply for a few hours so I moved onto the next mail.

The other session was for foot worship and he wanted to see me the following day. I replied saying I could do two pm and I needed a deposit to confirm.

As I re-read the first email I had a real niggling feeling that the mystery businessman visiting London could actually be François, after all I had put him on the spot. Could he be that serious that he would fly over to London just to see me and try and convince me? No, that would be crazy, there would be hundreds of girls like me in LA alone, why on earth would he fly half way round the world on a whim? Maybe I was just overthinking? Perhaps I needed a break?

I did a little more office work, tidied up my mailbox and closed the laptop as I prepared to take Russell for his morning walk. Just as I was putting on my boots my phone rang, it was the domme line. I looked at my watch, Jesus it wasn't even eight o'clock. I switched straight into my role.

"What the fuck do you want at this time in the morning?" I spat as I answered the call. Sometimes it was easy to be the bitch that these guys wanted, they were needy and had no respect for my personal time, case in point, which was pushing me to the limit some days and my temper was getting the better of me.

"Hi Mistress."

His voice sounded sly and I bit back at him.

"What do you want loser, it's too early for your pathetic games."

I could hear him doing you know what. For God's sake! It really was too early for this, why was my available schedule not working? He proceeded to tell me that he had his hard dick in a hoover, yes that is correct, he was using a hoover and sure enough if I listened carefully I could just about hear the noise of the vacuum cleaner in the background. For Christ's sake! I couldn't believe it, now I'd heard just about everything.

I started to laugh at him which was exactly what he wanted me to do but this time I wasn't acting as I formed the pictures in my head. Who wouldn't actually laugh at someone who had their knob stuck in a hoover? He wanted me to tell him how humiliating it was to think of a grown man sticking his member in a hoover and actually taking pleasure from it. And I answered his questions in great detail and promised that I would tell my friends about him. (You bet I would!)

This incredibly strange conversation with hoover dick lasted over forty minutes and by the end I was exhausted having to repeat myself constantly. All the time the noise of the vacuum cleaner persisted in the background and I sincerely believe he climaxed at least two or three times. I really had to wonder what the fuck was happening, it was surely not normal having to listen to this type of conversation at any time of day let alone before breakfast? I eventually let him go as he wanked himself furiously to another orgasm. I couldn't stand it anymore and even though I'd earned a bloody fortune so early in the day I wondered what was I doing and that surely there was more to life. Perhaps I did need a break and I thought more about the promised trip to LA and wondered whether I should contact François direct and put him on the spot.

During the afternoon I had a reply from the mystery business man. He stated he would be in the UK early next week and I asked him to send a deposit to confirm his appointment, and that was it. I would have to wait seven days to see if it was really him.

Strangely I hadn't heard from François via the usually email and phone calls and if I am honest I kind of missed having someone in my life that I spoke to on a daily basis. Oh God! What was happening? I was missing the contact from one of my clients, was I getting emotionally involved? Something I swore I would never do.

I decided to drop him an email to thank him for the overpriced shoes and the nice satin dress and asked why I hadn't heard from him. He replied and said that he'd been busy with work and that he would be busy over the next week but ended by saying that there were plenty more gifts heading my way. What every girl wants to hear I suppose and although I was disappointed he hadn't just Skyped me I clung to the positives and hoped I'd hear from him soon. At times I felt that he'd cooled off and moved on. Perhaps that's what these men did and my rejection of his trip to LA hadn't helped.

Over the week I heard once more from hoover boy, which reminded me to redo my availability schedule, I saw a customer for foot fetish who proved to be amazing at massaging my little tootsies and raped a wallet of another client until his Mastercard hit its limit and he loved every second of the experience. All in all it was a nice peaceful week and I had earned good money but it was always in the back of my mind why François hadn't called.

I had the mystery businessman booked in for Monday lunchtime so I decided to spend Sunday relaxing at a health spa with my mother. As I lay in a lovely hot Jacuzzi I convinced myself that the businessman was not François and perhaps he had moved on. I had lost a good client and what had turned out to be something of a friend too.

My Mum was doing my head in, not the ideal companion to have chosen to take to the health spa because she was hell bent on knowing the ins and outs of my recent life and it was proving rather tiresome.

She went on and on about Edward asking what had happened and why it had it ended so abruptly.

"You seemed so fond of him dear."

"I was Mum, but I don't want to talk about it."

What bit of 'I don't want to talk about it' did Mum not understand?

She went on and on telling me to call him and stated that no matter what had happened things could always be put right again.

"I've moved on Mum, I don't want to talk about it," I said for the tenth time.

"Has he rung you since?" she asked?

I shook my head.

"A few texts Mum but nothing that would convince me he wanted to give it another go."

"He hasn't called at the house?" she inquired.

"No Mum."

And so on, we all know how inquisitive our dear Mums can be don't we? She was like a dog with a damn bone!

"He must have done something really bad Jessica, I've never seen you this determined." She said.

I nodded and then Mum looked me straight in the eye and asked.

"What did he do Jessica."

I'd had enough and just came out with it.

"I caught him getting his wood polished if you must know Mum."

"His wood polished?" she asked confused.

"Yes Mum, another girl."

"But I don't... "

And at last the penny dropped and everything seemed to fall in place. She looked utterly horrified.

"Okay Mum? So can we just leave it now?"

"Yes dear of course, I'm so sorry, I just, well, I just thought it might have had something to do with David."

I shook my head.

"No Mum."

Mum changed the subject immediately; it seemed she was none-too comfortable talking about wood polishing.

"Oh gosh, look, it's time for our facial, come on lets go."

It wasn't time yet but it was a swift move on Mum's part and as she climbed out of the Jacuzzi I couldn't help laughing at her. Dear old Mum, God how I loved her.

Monday had arrived. I was totally confused as I had Skyped with François over the weekend and he didn't let anything slip or reveal any last minute plans of a business trip so I figured I must have been reading the whole thing wrong. I was pleased that he had Skyped me and yet part of me was a little disappointed that I wouldn't be meeting him in person.

I got myself ready; I was to meet the customer in the bar of his hotel. I dressed very smart and elegantly, the hotel was one of the best in London and I looked forward to the lunch date in one of the best restaurants in the capital. After lunch he was to take me for 'a spot of shopping' as he had put it.

I arrived early, chose a table that looked out onto the busy street and ordered a green tea then sent an email from my mobile to the businessman's phone telling him I was downstairs. The bar was empty apart from a young Russian couple impeccably dressed, they were sharing a bottle of champagne and there was a business man reading the Financial Times. I studied him carefully, might that be him? I watched for a few minutes but his iPhone remained silent on the table.

My green tea arrived and I took a mouthful as I placed the cup onto the saucer. I glanced at my watch wondering how long it would take for my client to appear when suddenly I was aware that someone was blocking out the light.

He cleared his throat purposely and I looked up. The delicate bone china cup slipped from my grasp and half a cup of green tea spilled onto the white linen table cloth.

He was there, in front of me, François, smiling, with a huge bouquet of red roses and a little Chanel bag.

"Oh my God , what are you doing here?" I asked.

"You asked me to convince you, remember?"

For once I was speechless.

"Didn't you know it was me, honestly?"

I still couldn't find any words. His accent was so adorable, and in the flesh he was so sexy and commanded a real presence. I could feel a flush come over me

Eventually I composed myself and spoke.

"I kind of had a hunch but you gave nothing away when we last Skyped so I was unsure."

He placed the roses onto the table along with the Chanel bag.

"I hope you don't mind, I brought you a present and I was told that all English ladies like roses."

"Yes, thank you, it's so nice to see you. Do you really have business here?"

He grinned as he held out his hand and asked me to stand.

"Yes I have business, I have business with you and I hope it will be a very positive meeting. He let out a long whistle as he slowly twirled me around. Oh my gosh I was blushing again, what was going on, this wasn't like me.

I gently pulled my hand away.

"So you are here just to see me?"

He nodded.

"That's right, I'm here to try and convince you to come and spend a little time with me in LA."

I was struck dumb yet again as the enormity of what he'd done sunk in. This man had flown nearly six thousand miles to see me and my first thoughts were that when I split up with Edward he wouldn't even drive eight miles to come and see me. But he was just a client, a customer. I was confused.

"But first let us enjoy London, please sit down."

He ushered me back into my seat and sat down opposite me as he reached across the table for my hand and although I instinctively wanted to pull my hand away it was as if we were magnetically joined together. The waiter came over with fresh strawberries and an ice cold bottle of Cristal.

"I hope you haven't driven here today Zeta, I want you to have fun, you work far too hard and today is not about me or my fetish, it is about you my darling."

He called me Zeta. It sounded so wrong. He called me darling, which also sounded so wrong. What was going on?

"This is the start," he said as he pushed over the Chanel bag and beckoned for me to open it. I couldn't help myself; I reached in and pulled out a small box.

"You really shouldn't have," I said.

"Please just open it," he said, "I was out in Oxford Street early this morning and when I saw it I thought it would suit you just fine."

I was trembling as I opened it and the box revealed a beautiful diamond pendant on a delicate chain.

"François, you shouldn't have, really you shouldn't have."

"Hush my dear," he said. "I wanted to show you how serious I am, hence why I am here and this is a small gift because I wanted to give you something when we first met up."

I smiled; he was such a nice person, not just the gifts I meant in general. He was a lovely kind person and then I remembered that he was my client and that for several weeks now I had abused and taunted him on camera. This wasn't sitting right with me at all.

We sat for over an hour before François announced we were going shopping. He spotted my discomfort immediately.

"Oh no, Zeta," he said. "Not that. I said today wasn't about me or my fantasies, this is about you, this is a normal shopping trip, just a couple of little things, we'll take in the sights and then we can go to dinner if that's okay with you?"

I breathed a huge sigh of relief. I'd had many real time sessions with clients after countless Skype sessions and had no problem with it whatsoever but somehow with François, it seemed different. I couldn't quite describe it but it was as if I'd lost the ability to act my part and I had an overwhelming urge to be myself.

As we left the hotel he hailed a cab and we headed to The Mall as he'd always wanted to see Buckingham Palace. It was a nice warm day and as we strolled through St James's Park I suddenly became aware of all the courting couples. I felt uneasy; this felt strange, it wasn't what I was used to. He didn't want me to act but there was no way I could just be me, Jessica! 'He's a customer' I murmured to myself as I instantly regretted having put myself in this situation.

I looked up at him, he was taking in the sites like a tourist but thank goodness didn't pick up on how uncomfortable I was.

"François," I said.

"Yes Zeta."

"Shall we move on somewhere else? Maybe a coffee?"

I suddenly felt the need to escape what seemed like a romantic atmosphere before I started to quietly freak out.

François smiled.

"You're the boss my dear," he teased.

The rest of the day was very pleasant, and if I'm very honest, I did try and entertain his fetish in a very small way while we were shopping, I very subtly flirted with the sales boy for my own sanity. I just wanted to feel in control I guess and out the corner of my eye I could see François' mouth open then close then he bit on his lip. I felt better immediately and decided to cut the shopping trip short and get some sightseeing done. From Buckingham Palace we went on the London Eye and then on to the restaurant L'Autre Pied in Blandford Street. François chose it; I guess it was quite apt for a man with a French background and I must say it was a first class choice, with classy modern European décor and food to die for. We took it easy and lingered there until early evening, my God I don't think I've ever stayed that long in a restaurant but the waiters seemed perfectly happy as François stretched the five courses out as long as he wanted.

I was more than a little tipsy as we walked down Blandford Street towards Marble Arch. It was that uncomfortable time, we'd had a great day and I had thoroughly enjoyed his company and we'd had so much in common but was there a sting in the tail? Was he about to come onto me and suggest a nightcap back at his hotel? I really hoped François would remember this was still business.

François was the perfect gentlemen as he put me into a taxi and placed a fifty pound note into the cabbie's hand.

"Can we meet up tomorrow?" he asked politely.

"Of course we can François; I'd like that very much."

And then he was gone.

I threw myself into the back seat of the taxi and sighed. Although confused, I had never felt so good in a long time.

Chapter Sixteen

I slept like a baby that night and awoke like a different girl. I was actually looking forward to meeting up with François again and dispensed with my normal daily routine which was a cup of coffee while checking through the emails that had come in through the night.

My mobile rang, I looked at my watch. It was before ten to eight in the morning for God's sake. It was the domme line... Oh no.

"Hello?" I answered.

"Hello Mistress I wondered if you could be so kind and talk to me?"

"Fuck off and die loser."

"Yes Mistress, that's perfect, that's what I want to hear."

"I meant it, now fuck off!"

I pressed 'end call'. Not altogether very professional but who cares I thought.

The truth was I couldn't wait to get over to Green Park and try and get to the bottom of François' plan to take me to LA. He'd mentioned something about talking business the evening before and I wanted to hear exactly what he had to say. The LA trip was very much on my mind now that I had actually met him in person.

I met François in the bar again. He was dressed a little more casual this time with a pair of blue jeans and an open neck white shirt which showed off his LA tan. I felt a little overdressed in my usual 'work' attire but nevertheless he made me feel at ease by commenting on how good I looked as he gave me a small peck on the cheek.

And then François surprised me by getting straight down to business coming right out with his request for me to fly back to LA with him.

He said he enjoyed cuckold but was unsure about anything else that went with it, for example the humiliation side of it. He kept asking me to fly out to LA and try out a real time fantasy of being his girlfriend but blatantly flirting with hot young men and either going off to another bar or club with them and carrying on from there. He said that he would book my ticket as soon as I agreed and he was willing to stay over in London for several more days to help me sort things out. I said the first excuse that came into my head.

"What about my dog?"

"Pardon?"

"My dog, I couldn't leave him behind."

François laughed. "Now I know how special you are. Is that the most important thing in your life?"

I nodded. He was.

François leaned across and quite suddenly the dynamic between us changed as he stroked my thigh. I jumped back in my seat not knowing what the hell was going on, how dare he act so intimate, he was a customer for Christ sake. He saw the look on my face and slowly pulled his hand away.

"I know this is confusing, I know I am confusing! I totally respect that you deal with people who know their place and I guess you may say black and white when it comes to their fantasy or fetish, but I struggle with it."

I looked at him, he was being so honest and sincere and at that moment I was beginning to understand what he wanted.

"I want you to come out to LA for a month," he said. "You will have your own room in my house, it will be a business transaction, no more. I'll pay you well and if you want to bring Russell with you I think we can make that happen."

He asked me if the dog had a pet passport and if his injections were up to date. They were.

"That's great then," he said. "It's my understanding that he needs to be checked by a vet and then wait seven or ten days thereafter but there are no great quarantine issues between the US and the UK though he does have to be flown in the hold with the luggage."

Russell in the hold with the luggage! Oh no!

François saw the change in my demeanour and was already trying to reassure me.

"Don't worry he won't freeze to death," he laughed. "They're monitored constantly throughout the flight though he will be given a tranquilizer to help him sleep."

Suddenly I felt a whole lot better and LA was beginning to sound like a possibility. We got down to practicalities and how I was worried that my business would surely suffer if I spent a month in Los Angeles. He accepted that and offered to write me a cheque, there and then for twenty thousand pounds that would cover any shortfalls.

His manner, the control he seemed to have over me was different to any other customer I had had before and I was starting to realise that although he liked the idea of cuckold fantasy role play all other parts of our days together, he took control. I thought back to yesterday, he had taken control of everything, that's why I was so taken aback and confused. He had liked it when I flirted with the sales boys but apart from that he was very much a man's man.

"That's it," I murmured.

He had chosen the shops, the restaurant, the champagne, the places we went to like tourists, even the clothes I bought he had chosen saying he liked them. Things were beginning to slip into place as I realised if I went to LA I wouldn't be in full control except for when it came to the other men. Okay, so most things like the credit cards, car and separate bedrooms would all be in my favour but the daily running of my life seemed to already be in François' hands and as I was only just piecing all this information together I was a little unsure as how to proceed. Should I just go with it I thought? Surely it would make my life a little easier as I wouldn't have to make decisions, just kind of turn up and flirt outrageously with other men and act like a bitch every now and then.

I must confess that throughout the conversation he took over from that point and any objections I had were quickly taken care of and everything he said made sense. There was no earthly reason why I shouldn't at least give it a try and yet deep down inside the thought of acting out François' cuckold fantasies for thirty days was about as appealing as watching paint dry. Surely the best actress or actor in the world couldn't act twenty four hours a day and I hung on a very simple sentence he'd said a little earlier, give it a try he'd said, and try out a real time fantasy of being his girlfriend for a month.

Okay, suppose I could handle that, what then? What if he loved it, where do you go from there? This sounded absolutely insane when I actually thought about what we were arranging to do. This wasn't normal – not normal at all. That was what was worrying me.

We spent the day mooching around, more touristy stuff, a little shopping and lunch again but this time François was very much in business mode, the business of persuading Zeta to fly out to LA after him the following week. I was feeling mixed up as my emotions ran away with me but over lunch I somehow agreed that I would give it a go and he seemed so pleased. I knew it would be hard to go back on my word.

I didn't want to commit to François full time, even during the time he spent in London. I always tried to keep him at arm's length and made no secret of the fact I was continuing to work while he was in London. This was a reminder of how crazy it was going to be in LA. How the hell was I going to go through with this?

François was leaving in two days and I had simply said I would give it a go I reassured myself, hell I don't even have to get on that damn plane if I don't want to!

I brought myself back to reality as I suddenly remembered where I was. I was in a beautiful hotel room not far from François' hotel. I sat by the window looking out over the rat race below. The curtains were a rich gold and hung the full height of the luxuriously decorated room. I was sitting on a large gold, velvet, ornate chair with my feet up and resting on a man on all fours as I read a magazine and sipped on a fresh coffee.

I took a moment to look at him, his head hung towards the floor as he performed his duty of my footstool. Yes you heard correctly he was my foot stool that is all he wanted. I had received an email for a real time session and he said he wanted to act as

169

human furniture. To be honest I was a little curious so decided to go for it. The submissive was not allowed to talk unless answering me back, and later if everything went well he might make a request that he could be my seat too.

It was harmless enough I thought so arranged a time and day with him and here we were. He treated me like a Goddess and had ordered chocolate, champagne and coffee.

He was already staying at the hotel on business and had asked politely if I would be able to come to him in between his meetings. As soon as I had walked into the room he'd got down onto all fours and as I made myself comfortable he inched over towards me. There didn't appear to be anything to worry about and he seemed to be taking his role as my furniture very seriously. I smiled to myself as he asked if he could kiss my feet as a sign of my superiority. I agreed and he crawled up closer to me on his hands and knees and started to kiss my shoes. He spent two or three minutes doing that and then handed me the menu saying that I must be hungry. It was only ten in the morning so I asked if he could order some fresh orange juice and pastries.

"Along with the coffee already here that will be perfect, thank you," I smiled.

"I am so glad you are pleased Mistress," he bowed and picked up the phone making my order.

As soon as he had put the phone down he was back on his hands and knees and my feet were back resting in the small of his back. I got out my mobile and started to reply to some emails, around twenty minutes later I looked down.

"Okay slave?" I asked.

"Mistress, may I please pamper you?" he stammered still looking at the floor. I took my feet off his back allowing him to get up. He disappeared into the large marble bathroom where I could hear the taps turn on. He scurried back into the open plan room bringing with him three or four flannels, removed my stilettos and started massaging my feet with sweet smelling oils which he then washed off with the hot flannels. It was quite the most exquisite treatment my feet have ever had. In between the oil treatment he produced an array of magazines for me to read, Vogue, Tatler and more. I battled with the thoughts of LA that now seemed to loom over me like a large storm cloud, this was my life and it suited me just fine I thought to myself. I was enjoying every minute of the session but as usual I couldn't show how pleased I actually was because he was my little slave and that was exactly how he wanted me to be treated, praise and niceties were off limits.

As soon as the knock on the door came he excused himself and opened the door as if it was the most normal thing in the world. He stood there, bare chested in the dog collar as the poor girl pushed in the large silver trolley. Give her her due, she was a true professional and never gave him a second look.

The submissive was clearly enjoying his tasks and for the first time I could see the bulge in his pants. He served me more coffee and as I eyed the boner I told him off.

Straight away he was down on his knees apologising. "Please forgive me Mistress, it's so revolting for you to see that, oh please forgive me."

"Calm down slave," I said, "just pour me another coffee and then get back down on your knees so I can rest my feet; that way that boner of yours is out of my sight."

I sat there with my feet up and was half way through Vogue when I remembered I had to use him as a human chair so I stood up and walked closer to the huge windows again.

"I want to sit here," I announced and without having to say anything else he scuttled over and I sat down on him. After around five minutes I demanded a drink so that he would have to be relieved of his task. As he stood up his erection was still clearly visible. I told him he was a naughty slave and he apologised profusely.

As he came back with the orange juice I took a hold of him by the collar.

"You've had that hard on for some time now slave. Why don't you do something about it?"

"Oh no Mistress, I most certainly couldn't, not in your presence."

"Really?" I questioned, more than a little puzzled.

"We are near the end of our session," I said. "You don't want to treat yourself?"

He was pouring a little champagne into the orange juice. I gave him a shrug of the shoulders, a suit yourself type of look when he told me he had a thing for stockings or tights and he would be eternally grateful if I could leave some with him as I left. He blushed scarlet and looked at the floor as he handed me my Buck's Fizz.

What the hell I thought, he paid me well so what was a spare pair of stockings. I rummaged in my oversized bag and pulled out a spare pair I kept for occasions just like that, a cheap pair but he wasn't to know that. I threw them at him, told him to knock himself out. I gave him a wink and gathered my coat and chose a magazine to take to relax with in the bath later that day. He wanted to book me for next month but of course I told him to email me.

Chapter Seventeen

François was leaving the next day, so I was meeting him to finalise everything for the following week when I was supposed to fly out with Russell and start our strange arrangement. Up until now there had been no role plays and he had treated me like a lady, and I had allowed that. If I am honest with you I was enjoying it. As I had pieced together what information I could about how he handled this fantasy of his I understood that he liked to treat me well. We had lunches in some superb restaurants and he literally bought me a new wardrobe for my 'business trip' to LA. I had fought against this as in my mind it was still an unsure deal, I was still going back and forth in my thoughts and quite frankly I was sick to death of thinking about it. Seeing the pile of clothes made me feel sick, it made me feel like I HAD to go, like I had no choice, a feeling I was really not used to.

With François leaving the next day he requested a real time cuckold session. I saw it coming and could understand why because the question of sex or any type of sexual release had never been mentioned. François was a man, he had needs and to the best of my knowledge they had not been met, though there were many occasions where he could have disappeared into the city and satisfied his urges with some other girl.

He talked at length about how I had to act. He wanted to believe I was a kind of man-eating, powerful female who spent her days sweating her body into perfect shape at the gym followed by some sort of beauty treatment or hair appointment. I was to tell him all about the gym and then a make believe lunch and of course a date with a muscular overly handsome, wealthy stud resulting in a night of rampant porn star sex.

I found myself cringing at the reality of this fantasy person François perceived me to be. I was normal, what was wrong with that? I wanted to tell him that I woke up like most – still feeling tired and needing copious amounts of coffee to get me through the morning. François had never seen me first thing in the morning, he had never seen me without make up or clad in a designer dress. I half wanted to explain the reality that I had days when I wore no makeup and did laundry and grocery shopping. I wanted to tell him that I wasn't having any sex, let alone with hunky studs and that I went to bed solo with my little dog Russell and did not in fact look like a Victoria Secret model in the gym but just a girl obsessed with trying to burn off last night's binge of a 'share size' bag of Maltesers and half a bottle of red wine. I'd say I was more Bridget Jones than Angelina Jolie but of course he didn't want to hear that.

He handed me an envelope. Inside was one thousand pounds of crisp unused notes. So today we were each to play our roles. I smiled at him masking my disappointment.

"Let's go to lunch then," I said sternly, starting my role as his dominating bitch of a girlfriend. We headed to a popular restaurant where I proceeded to flirt with anything with a cock. It was a sorry sight but I could see straight away he was in his element. It brought me to realise that this is exactly what my life would be like in LA. It was a rude awakening and totally different to the days I'd had since François' arrival. The question I now asked myself was if I could live with François for a month, acting like this whenever I was in his company. Who would I talk to as me, Jessica? When could I just be myself? .

That day was all about teasing him and of course every other poor bloke in sight! By the time it came for me to get washed and changed I was exhausted. He had booked me a room to use to get freshened up and a nice body massage to thank me for my day's work, or so I thought. When I opened the door an extremely handsome rather large man was standing there smiling.

"Good evening miss, I'm here to help start your relaxing evening."

I was totally taken a back and hoped to God this straightforward massage was all François had in mind. I'm sure François wouldn't put me in the position that was currently flying through my mind, it felt like the start to a cheap lurid porno and I sure as hell wouldn't be participating in it.

I smiled and stepped aside as the hunk entered the room.

"Um, great, that's just great."

The fake and slightly horrified smile was plastered all over my face and I'm sure he spotted it a mile off as he set up a portable bench in the middle of the room and covered it with a large towel. He interrupted my thoughts

"I have set up Miss, so I will leave you to unrobe. A Swedish massage followed by an Indian head massage has been booked for you, however you are welcome to change the treatments if you so wish."

I started to relax realising this was actually just a complimentary massage with an overly fine gorgeous specimen at my service. The masseur said he'd give me a few minutes and he'd leave the door unlocked. Five minutes later he was back with yes, you guessed it, a bottle of champagne. This was amazing, I thought, LA was calling me and beginning to appeal once again. Whatever doubts were going through my mind, one thing was for certain, François knew how to push the boat out.

Later that night we went over the details of the proposal, it was pretty much all in my favour but I was still slightly unsure. I would live in his house but not share a bedroom, I would have my own car and if I wished a driver and he'd give me my own credit cards and of course regular shopping trips with him. He told me how much he had enjoyed our session as his 'bitch cheating girlfriend' as he so nicely put it, I faked a big smile and sipped on my drink. FUCK! I was so confused and the clock was ticking, my time would soon be up.

Chapter Eighteen

As we pulled up to the airport in the hotel's car François turned to look at me.

"Russell is all sorted for his journey to LA, you have the money for your ticket, it's all systems go!" he smiled. He looked so happy, his eyes danced as he squeezed my hand.

I had the dreaded sick feeling in the pit of my stomach as my mind raced.

"Yes, it sure is."

I faked a smile and quickly pulled my hand away reaching for the door and getting out.

Once outside the car he again tried to hold my hand.

"I hope you don't change your mind Zeta, everything is sorted, all you have to do is get on the plane next week!"

"I won't," I replied, unsure myself if that answer was a lie or not. I wanted to go so much, I liked him as a person, I had grown fond of him, I just didn't want to go over there to be Zeta! Perhaps...

"It's Jessica," I blurted out as he took the luggage trolley from the chauffeur, "not Zeta."

He looked at me stunned but the look on his face said that it meant a lot that I had shared it with him.

"That's such a lovely name, and it suits you," he smiled. "I really can't wait for next week Jessica," he blushed taking a quick glance at his watch.

"I have to go and check in, this is for you."

He handed me a manila envelope.

"It has all my contact details, including my secretary and office lines, any problems or questions just call me, please! She knows about you, she knows you're special to me. Now I have to go."

He took my hand and kissed it gently then he was gone.

When I got back home I put on my walking boots and left my phone in the house in the bid to get some clarity on this fucked up situation. I still came to the same conclusion. I wanted to go but I didn't want to go as Zeta. But on the other hand maybe if I did go and we continued to get on like we had perhaps he would be willing to give up on the whole silly scenario he lusted after and want to get to know me as me.

The week flew by. I had a vet's appointment for Russell and a load of sessions booked in before I supposedly jetted off for a month. I had told Mum I was going for a holiday and meeting friends over there. I hardly think telling the truth in this instance was the right thing to do. I could see it now 'well Mum, the thing is I accidently became a dominatrix, and some rich guy flew over from LA to try and persuade me to follow him over there and be his fake girlfriend that has her wicked way with lots of young studs which in turn makes him extremely aroused and I've decided to go for it – see you in a month'! Hmmm yes I think a white lie works perfectly in this occasion!

I was packed and ready. D-day was here. My flight was at eleven thirty that morning and I had to be there at least three hours before to sort out Russell and check in. Of course François had been in constant contact for the last week making sure I was still thinking of coming. He was being pushier which only had me more anxious. I sat in the cab with Russell in his carry case, everything was a blur, the cab ride, my thoughts, even the last week! Nothing was making sense. Was I really going to LA to try and get François to kind of fall for the real me? Is that what I was doing? Fuck! I started to panic as the driver pulled into the departures drop off.

"Here we are madam," he opened my door and proceeded to take my luggage out of the boot.

Oh my God why couldn't I have met a normal person I liked? Why did it have to be so fucking complicated? I was so angry with myself. I was the only person to blame. I should have just said no to this whole stupid offer right from the word go. What was I thinking?

"Miss, Miss are you okay?"

The taxi driver was now staring at me totally freaked out.

"Oh my gosh, I'm so sorry. Sorry... how much did you say?"

I paid the taxi driver and walked into the airport trying to find the BA check-in desks. Russell started crying as streams of travellers and workers bustled by.

"What shall I do?" I murmured looking around, Russell's cries were getting louder as security announcements and final calls boomed overhead.

I quickly moved out of the way to a quiet spot and slumped between my case and the wall pulling his carry case onto my lap and looked around waiting for my brain to function.

Suddenly my pocket started vibrating as my phone rang, I pulled it out.

It was the domme line. Shit! I had forgotten to deactivate it. I answered it.

"Hello Mistress, can we talk?"

"Fuck off!"

"Oh thank you Mistress that makes me feel so good."

"I mean it, fuck off."

I pressed 'end' and as I did I stared over the top of the phone and a figure of a man slowly focused into view. He was somehow familiar to me. My throat tightened and I gasped for breath as I felt the hairs on the back of my neck stand on end and without being able to do anything about it I started to tremble.

"What are you doing here?"

"I'm on business," he said.

That figured, he was always on business, how else could he afford the best of everything including a private chauffeur? Strangely enough I didn't have the urge to claw his eyes out and I even felt my mouth forming into a slight smile.

"What sort of business?" I asked. "Where are you heading for?"

Edward shrugged his shoulders.

"I don't know yet. It depends where you are heading off to."

Was this his idea of a little joke?

"I'm not with you," I said. "You're in departures so you must be going somewhere."

"My business is to win you back so wherever you're going I'm going to book the very next flight."

Edward was playing with me right? Some kind of sick mind game. I thought back to the last time I had seen him and all of a sudden that horrible sick feeling surfaced once again. Maybe I did want to claw out his eyes after all.

"Look Edward, I'm incredibly stressed out and heading for LA on some business of my own so if you don't mind I could really do without this and I've got less than half an hour to check Russell in."

I stood, took a few steps forward and tried to push past him but he stood his ground.

"I've been to a therapist Jess, I've changed."

"What?"

"It's true Jess," he said. "I was obsessed with sex, I didn't know what it was to say no and I've realised what you meant to me. Please give me another chance; I'll do anything for you."

My head was spinning.

"You fucking followed me here to tell me that?"

"Sort of," he said, "a friend of yours happened to let slip that you were heading off to the States and I had someone watching you and he gave me a call earlier today when he saw you walking out of your house with a couple of suitcases."

"You had me followed?"

"A private detective."

"You fucking bastard, you had no right."

He took a step forward and I slapped him as hard as I could in the face.

I called him more names as people started to take notice around us. I didn't care. I told him how much he'd hurt me. I said he was feeble and weak and didn't even have the balls to turn up at my house to try and win me back. I told him too much water had flowed under the bridge and that a leopard never changes its spots and that he was out of order having me followed.

He looked pitiful as he mumbled something about changing and some therapist from Harley Street when I'm sure I saw a tear in his eye. But I left him standing on his own as I located the BA helpdesk and soon after as I bid a tearful farewell to poor Russell I made my way to the BA VIP lounge, a concession that came with my first class ticket.

I'm glad the alcohol was included because with the amount I consumed I think I would have needed to take a small bank loan to cover my bill. I was in there for over two hours and believe me I took full advantage of the 'freebies' on offer. I tried a smoked salmon salad too, but after the first two forkfuls had passed over my lips I felt like vomiting. I was annoyed that Edward had affected me like that.

My flight had been announced and a pretty young girl in an immaculate BA uniform walked over and told me I needed to make tracks. I'm glad she did because I had heard nothing, my mind turning cartwheels. The alcohol did the trick for the first few hours as I slept like a baby but then I woke up with the headache from hell which seemed to be compounded with the altitude and somewhere across the Atlantic I burst into tears.

The cabin staff were magical. Thankfully the first class seats beside me were empty and one flight attendant, a young girl called Toni sat down with me for about twenty minutes while I blurted out my sorry tale. She fed me with black coffee and I told her everything, and I mean everything. I'm not sure if she thought I was telling the truth or if I'd shocked her into silence but she was a good listener. I came to the scene in the airport when Edward had appeared and her jaw dropped open with surprise.

She pressed a button above her head and seconds afterwards a colleague of hers stood over us.

"What is it Toni?" she asked.

"Get me a large gin and tonic," she said.

As the stewardess walked away Toni spoke.

"So let me get this right. You're flying out to spend a month with a guy who gets off on you being the bitch from hell, talking to him about spending nights with well hung young studs and at the same time telling him how inadequate he is."

"Yes."

"And you think you might be developing feelings for him though you are not entirely convinced and if those feelings do develop you would like to get to the bottom of this errr... obsession of his and even try to overcome it?"

"That is correct."

"And if you do, you're wondering if it's possible to have a normal, physical relationship with this François?"

"Yes."

"And as you were leaving for LA this perfect Edward guy makes an appearance, a man who you were absolutely besotted with but the last time you saw him he was um, having fun with another girl, and he says he's sorry and that he was a sex addict but he's sought professional help and now he says he's cured and he wants you back?"

"Yes."

Toni leaned back in her seat and drained the last of her drink.

"What do you think?" I asked.

Toni whistled as she shook her head. "I think you should put that all in a book because it would be a bestseller for sure."

Toni stood.

"Wait," I said. "What should I do?"

"What should you do?" she said, looking exasperated. "I haven't a bloody clue my dear."

François was waiting for me as I completed the overlong US passport interrogation and made my way through the masses of people. There were dozens of people holding up boards with company names and surnames of strangers coming into the country. As I walked towards him I couldn't help breaking out into a big beaming smile. He looked so handsome and at that point I realised how much I had missed him even though it had only been a week since he had left London.

He took both my hands in his and stared at me.

"You look beautiful Jessica."

"You don't look so bad yourself," I joked, and yet I wasn't because François looked gorgeous.

The LA sun had put a little colour into his cheeks and I swore he even looked a little younger.

It was just over an hour's drive to his house and it looked exactly like it had in the photographs he had sent me. He showed me to my own room which was the size of an average London apartment. It had an en-suite and an open plan lounge area with a small kitchen and French doors that opened out onto the pool and a small covered gym. It was like something out of the movies, it took my breath away. François then gave me the guided tour, introduced me to the housekeeper and then the gardener who was tidying up the garage.

François was fussing around me like a long lost daughter he hadn't seen for ten years and told me time and again that he was so pleased I'd made the journey. That night we sat down to a wonderful welcoming meal the housekeeper had prepared earlier. He opened a special bottle of champagne that I wanted to refuse due to the amount of alcohol I'd consumed in Gatwick but it didn't seem right as François was so excited.

After three hours I was feeling the strain. Although I'd slept for a couple of hours on the plane that was the only rest I'd had in nearly thirty hours. I almost fell asleep at the table and finally François escorted me to my bedroom.

I dreamt of Edward, I dreamt of the good times we'd had together and cursed him when I awoke the following morning. However, I felt refreshed and ready for what life was about to throw at me, whatever the hell that might be given the circumstances.

I found François in the pool as he explained his usual routine was to swim a hundred lengths followed by a little breakfast. The housekeeper was busy at the far end of the pool fussing around a table that had been set under a bamboo pergola. It was idyllic, what a way to start a day and I promised to join François for a swim the next morning.

We were half way through breakfast when François spoiled everything and reminded me why I was there. He presented me with a timetable he had prepared detailing the days and times of our real time role plays. It was as if somebody had kicked me in the stomach as he brought me back down to earth with a bump.

After breakfast he took me upstairs and into his bedroom where my outfit had been laid out on the bed. There was a rather tight looking flesh coloured dress with a brand new pair of matching Christian Louboutins and an oversized large red handbag. Lying on the pillow were several items of gold jewellery which completed the look. He had clearly taken a lot of care and attention to detail and I couldn't help but be a little impressed as I looked at him and gave him an approving smile. He told me he had to attend to a little business for a few hours but that I needed to be ready by one thirty and he would be taking me to one of the most popular eateries in LA, The Polo Lounge. I frowned as

I eyed up the dress, I would clearly not be indulging in much eating judging by the size of it. That was all well and good and this was what he was paying me for but I wanted more, I wanted to see more of the man I'd first met in London. I wanted François to play the tour guide and at least show me a little bit of LA before we fell into our roles.

It wasn't to be. At one thirty exactly François knocked on my bedroom door and a big smile pulled across his face when he was greeted by his 'bitch.' And so it started. My 'bitch' frown was there from the outset (as instructed) as I cursed his choice of restaurant, what he was wearing, the position of the table he'd chosen and of course his choice of food. And when the food arrived and the waiter stood over us I went into my over the top tantrum and made reference to the fuck of my life I'd had the previous evening with my stud from the local American football team. François revelled in it, he squirmed with discomfort but he revelled in it and then half way through the main course I broke down and sobbed like a child.

François didn't know what to do at first but he quickly took control, paid the bill and then got me out of there as quick as he could. The drive back home was more or less in silence but the enquiry started soon after. I was honest with François. I told him that my feelings for him had developed in London. He was sympathetic and I think quite pleased that he had had that effect on me but as I told him I was finding it difficult to combine the two roles his face was etched with disappointment.

"I can't do it François." I said. "It's okay with my regular clients but you have become more than a regular client and I feel like I want something normal with you."

François stuttered. "Normal... what do you mean normal? This is normality to me, it turns me on; you know that."

"Well it's not normal to me," I said.

We talked for hours. I said that fetishes were fine as long as they didn't inflict any pain or discomfort on the participants but that's what they were... fetishes and there was no harm in a little role play now and again but not at the expense of the sexual act of intercourse, that all important bond between husband and wife, partners and lovers.

Poor François poured his heart out as he explained everything, taking me back to when he was a small boy of fourteen.

"My cousins were from Kansas; let's just say they were born on the wrong side of the tracks after my Uncle Tony took up with a part time hooker he met in a bar in the city. My father did his best to warn him but he took to drugs and drink and before he knew it she had her claws into him and after a crazy forty eight hour drink and drug fuelled binge one weekend they thought it a good idea to get hitched and they did."

I sat and listened in amazement and I kept silent.

"The two of them were killed when Uncle Tony drove across the railway tracks one night after a particularly heavy session. He didn't hear or see the train that cut the car in two and they found what was left of their bodies half a mile up the tracks when the train came to a halt."

François reached for the coffee I had made him as he continued.

"My father insisted Laura and Caroline came to live with us."

"Your uncle's daughters?" I asked.

"Yes. Twins, six months older than me but a million light years more advanced."

I guessed exactly where this was going, at last I was going to get to the bottom of exactly where François' fetish had originated and I kind of guessed the finale even before it had begun.

"Some would say it was every schoolboy's dream but it didn't start that way." François wiped at a tear in the corner of his eye before resuming.

"The first time it happened Mom and Dad had been staying over at a friend's house. They guessed we were old enough to be left overnight on our own. They had been out for an hour or so when Laura appeared naked in the lounge. She danced and pranced around a little and then Caroline joined her giggling like schoolgirls, which of course they were. It was clearly planned and they knew exactly what they were doing."

François described how they had eventually turned their attention to him and before long the three of them were naked and the two cousins almost fought over François' erection.

"I didn't last long. Laura had managed to guide me inside her and within what seemed like only seconds I had ejaculated."

François' lip was trembling as he continued.

"And that was when the abuse started. They told me I was fucking useless and Caroline led me round the room by my dick as they laughed and ridiculed me. They told me what a hopeless specimen I was and that I would never be a real man with a cock that size. And then something strange happened."

I looked at François and managed to bite my lip.

"I started to get hard again and a smile pulled across Caroline's face as she realised it was her turn next and she took full advantage as she squatted on me and rode me like there was no tomorrow. I was able to last longer this time, which I confess made me feel a whole lot better. I was a virgin at the time and yet within the space of fifteen minutes I'd had full sexual intercourse with two girls and I felt like a superhero."

I finished the story for François.

"So it was a regular occurrence every time you found yourself alone in the house with the two of them."

François nodded.

I continued.

"The verbal abuse became part of the sexual act and within time you needed that abuse just to get aroused?"

"Yes," he said. "They seemed to look on it as a game and within a very short time they started to verbally abuse me from the outset and of course the more they abused me the quicker I got hard. Eventually it got to the stage where I couldn't get erect without the abuse."

"But surely you had more sexual experiences with other girls?" I asked.

"Yes," François said. "Twice, both times disasters. I couldn't get hard even when one girl took me in her mouth and worked on me for a ten minutes."

Poor François said that his lack of being able to perform filtered back to the classroom and he was made to feel like a laughing stock all over again. He said how had plucked up the courage to visit a few prostitutes in his early twenties but with the same results each time.

"The problem is in your head," I said.

François started to laugh.

"What is it?" I asked puzzled.

"You don't get it do you?"

"Get what?" I said.

"You think I have a problem, but I don't see it that way. I can get aroused, maintain an erection and come whenever I choose too so where's the problem. Some men watch porn... "

I jumped in.

"Of course there's a problem François, you're only masturbating, you don't know what it's like to bond sexually with someone you care for. Your pervy little cousins abused you and they've deprived you of so much."

At that point François hung his head. I made myself a promise that I would help him to overcome his problem because that's what it was. All of a sudden my thoughts drifted back to all the clients I'd engaged with in the past. Something had to have happened to them somewhere along the way. What the hell makes a man force sandwiches down his throat in order to achieve an orgasm? How the hell can a man get turned on getting custard pies thrown into his face?

The early evening sun was setting on the far end of the pool and we caught the last of the rays as the heat warmed our bodies. François said he felt a whole lot better now that he'd managed to talk to someone about what had happened. I said it was a start, nothing more than that, but tomorrow was another day and we'd take the next step together.

We shared a bed that night. There was no sex, not even a sign of any foreplay nor did we kiss but I fell asleep in his arms and it felt good. He was downstairs in the kitchen when I eventually awoke and I heard Russell snoring loudly at the bottom of the bed. He was fast asleep on a rather expensive chaise longue. François had made a little breakfast and told the housekeeper to take the day off. It felt like a new beginning he said and I felt exactly the same. I knew it wasn't going to be easy but if there was just a remote possibility of building something resembling a normal relationship with François then I was willing to try.

Chapter Nineteen

So why the hell did Edward have to show up and throw a spanner in the works?

It was two days later when François walked over to me as I lay by the pool and told me there was someone at the intercom on the gates asking for me by name. Before François even mentioned his name I knew exactly who it was.

"He said he is called Edward and he's very persistent and he wants to see you."

I was momentarily speechless, a whole host of emotions coursing through my body. I was angry, I was certainly angry because a huge part of me still hadn't forgiven Edward for what he had done to me. While I didn't want to admit it to anyone I still hadn't got over that fateful day when I'd caught Edward cheating and there was even more anger inside me because he hadn't had the balls to come and face me and at least try to explain where it had all gone wrong. I found myself thinking back to what he had said at the airport about seeking help. And then a moment of weakness as someone inside me whispered that he may not have ventured over to the other side of town when he had cheated but here he was, and he'd flown halfway across the planet to explain himself.

"Shall I call the cops?" François had interrupted my thoughts.

"No, please no, he's a friend François."

"Fine," he said, "I'll buzz him in then and he can have a coffee with us."

"No," I shouted.

François shrugged his shoulders.

"Make your mind up Jess and tell me what I should do because I swear he'll be climbing the fucking gate if we don't make a decision soon."

I climbed from the sun bed and pulled a robe around me.

"I'll go to the gates."

"What does he want Jessica?"

"I don't know, I'll find out."

It was over two hundred metres to the gate; it was the longest walk of my life. Edward stood patiently with two hands on the bars of the large ornate gate.

"Now I know what you would look like in prison." I quipped.

He smiled... that beautiful smile I remembered so well.

"I deserve prison time after what I did to you," he said.

I shook my head as I reached the gate.

"Don't be stupid, you're a man and that's what men do, they scheme and cheat and plot because it's in their genes to do so."

"I can't argue with that," he said, "but I swear I've had help and I've worked it out."

I promised to meet Edward in his hotel the following day and then he left. I told François the truth. That he was an ex-boyfriend who had cheated on me. He had found out from a friend that I was here in LA and that he was here on business.

François quizzed me a little. He asked if Edward would be staying in LA long, I said no even though I was unaware of his plans – other than to win me back of course. I decided to keep that to myself! I told François that I had promised to have some lunch with him in his hotel. He looked a little upset, dare I say even jealous. Jesus H Christ what a quandary, a cheating bastard of an ex-boyfriend who had chased me half around the world and a cuckold client who got off on abuse and was actually starting to fall for me. What a complete mess!!!

That night François dropped a bombshell and told me that he thought he was in love with me and that he would move heaven and earth in order to form a normal relationship with me... if that's what I wanted?

I found myself nodding. François looked so happy as he told me that he had booked his first session with a therapist. Bloody hell! Therapists for François, therapists for Edward! And it was me who was responsible for both. I felt torn between the devil and the deep blue sea.

Edward knew everything there was to know about sex addiction and by the time he took me to lunch I was feeling quite educated on the subject. He quoted and cited various medical studies and reeled of countless names such as hypersexuality erotomania, paraphilia nymphomania, satyriasis, Don Juanism and compulsive sexual behaviour and he explained the detailed medical studies carried out by professional psychologists, sociologists, clinical sexologists and other specialists who on the whole agreed that sexual addiction was a medical, physiological, and psychological addiction.

At first I thought he was talking BS but the more he talked and quoted and referred to studies that could be found online I found myself believing every word he said.

He persuaded me to take a light lunch in his hotel's restaurant and he continued his analysis of what had happened.

"We all have the brain reward circuitry that makes food and in particular sex, rewarding," he said. "It's a natural survival mechanism Jess, these rewards have feedback mechanisms which lead to the pathological pursuit of rewards and before we know it we are addicted and can't stop."

I held up a hand as I stopped him.

"Listen Edward, I can understand all that and I think your explanation of why you cheated on me carries a little merit, however you were well aware that you and I were fucking like little rabbits on heat when we were together and whenever you wanted me you only had to pick up the phone. In fact, on that ill-fated day I was on my way round to do just that, so how can you justify your actions?"

Edward was shaking his head.

"I can't Jess, it was wrong, I know it was but she threw herself at me and I couldn't say no and yet even though I hated myself for what I'd done I knew the next time it happened I would do exactly the same so that's why I had to get help. My therapist diagnosed hyper sexuality and said it's sometimes linked to compulsive and impulsive disorders."

"You never came near me until you decided to follow me to the airport," I said.

"I couldn't Jess, I would have fed you a boat load of promises I couldn't keep."

"You hurt me so badly."

"I'm sorry Jessica, I truly am but I'm different now, please believe me."

I stood up to leave. This was all getting to much for me and revisiting the past was not what I wanted to do. I'd fought my way through the pain and convinced myself I was stronger as a result. I could now feel the energy draining from my body and I needed to get away.

"I'm sorry Edward but this is all too much. I hear what you are saying and it sounds like a good excuse but it doesn't change anything."

"But Jessica I..."

"If it makes you feel better then I understand and I forgive you."

I picked up my bag and walked away from the table.

"But Jess, wait."

I turned around to face him.

"There you are; does that make you feel better? I forgive you, now you can book your flight back home – mission accomplished."

He took me by the arm as I reached the lobby and spun me round. Our faces were only inches apart and for the first time I smelled his expensive aftershave and it brought back the most delicious memories.

"My mission isn't accomplished at all," he whispered gently. "My mission is to win you back, to take you back home and to marry you and I want us to have children and grow old together. I love you more than you could ever imagine and if I have to stay in this hotel until this time next year then I'll do it."

They say that there comes a time where time stands still and it happened at that precise moment in the Hotel Casa Del Mar in Santa Monica. It was as if we were cocooned in our own private bubble. I was aware of people passing by, of telephones ringing at reception and voices of people having conversations yet in our secret world nothing happened. I couldn't breathe let alone speak. I hadn't imagined it; it was a wedding proposal of sorts, not the best or most romantic in the world but it was a defined statement of intent. The man whom I'd loved with all my soul, the man who once made my flesh tingle and caused my heart to skip a beat whenever he touched me had announced he wanted to marry me. He leaned in to me and made an attempt to kiss me. I wanted to pull away but something held me there. Our lips brushed, my head started to swim and my brain was suddenly filled with natural chemicals which made my whole body shudder with pleasure. Shit! I told myself, it was only a kiss; it shouldn't make me feel like this but it did and I responded and we kissed like no one in the world existed. It's difficult to gauge how long that kiss lasted but the first I knew about it was a big burly security guard tapping me on the shoulder warning us that we were about to be thrown out. Edward told him that he was a guest in the hotel and that he had a room. The security man smiled and then spoke.

"Then I suggest you use it sir."

To say I was embarrassed was an understatement. Eventually, after what seemed like an eternity I did the only thing I could think of... I ran like hell.

François took me out that evening and happily announced that he'd had his first session with his therapist and things couldn't have gone any better because for the first time in his life he sincerely believed it was possible to think about being able to have a normal sexual relationship. Perhaps not next week, he said, not even next month but he could see the light at the end of the tunnel and he would work at it harder than he had ever worked at anything before.

François reached across the table and took both my hands in his.

"I'll work it out Jessica," he said. "I've never met anyone like you before, I'm so lucky to have found you and believe me I'm not going to lose you. I want you to stay here permanently I don't want you to go back to England."

I wanted to object, offer up good reasons why I needed to be back in London but I couldn't think of any. This man loved me and he was willing to change his life just so that we could have a normal relationship. No man had come anywhere near doing this much for me and it touched me. I found myself nodding in agreement, thinking how well Russell had settled and how good my life would be. I didn't need the business I was involved with back home, didn't need men force feeding themselves with sandwiches just to be able to jack themselves off. I didn't need men calling me at eight in the morning or while shopping at Sainsbury's so that I could ridicule the size of their penis.

The more time I had spent with François the more I got to like him. He made me laugh; he made me feel good in myself and treated me with respect. If we could get the sex side of things on track who knows what might happen and by his own admission, today had been a big step forward for him.

The only person I'd really miss would be Mum but François' house was big enough to accommodate her. I'd fly her out for a month at a time as often as she wanted and we'd spend real quality time together.

As François leaned across the table and kissed me passionately for the first time I waited to float gently away into another world. I found myself torn between these two men. This was crazy, no man had ever come near me in three months and now I had kissed two in a day!

I dreamt that night and remembered every detail when I awoke as the sun streamed through the thin veiled curtains. I felt refreshed and ready to take on the world and yet the confusion seemed to be building inside me, it was growing by the minute. François and I took a pleasant breakfast at the pool and I enjoyed every minute as I tried to imagine that this would be what my life would be like on a permanent basis. Everything in the garden appeared rosy apart from the fact that I was thinking about Edward constantly.

I'm not a great believer in the law of attraction and yet it was quite surreal when just after noon, after thinking about Edward all morning, he showed up at the gate again. This time François was quite angry and I couldn't blame him.

"I'm calling the cops Jessica and I'm having this man thrown in jail. You said it was over between you and its obvious to me he's stalking you."

I remained silent and nervous. What a fucking mess. I walked to the gate with François as he confronted Edward and told him to clear off. I stood like a lemon as Edward begged me to tell François that he wasn't stalking me and that we were planning to get married.

I think that pissed me off a little. Edward had this strange habit of being able to say things that wound me up. I turned to François and shrugged my shoulders.

"The man is clearly delusional," I said. "I think you should call the cops."

François nosed right up to the bars of the gate and this time he was shouting. "Jessica is in a relationship with me buddy, so I think you should take your ass out of here."

Edward looked astonished.

"Tell him the truth Jess; tell the old bastard the truth."

Well, if before I was angry, Edward had just pushed me into the furious camp. There was absolutely no need to call François that, even though he was a good fifteen years older than Edward. Still he ranted on outside the gates while François picked up his phone and dialled the police. The conversation that took place between them was almost comical.

"Let me in, I need to speak to my fiancé."

François wore the biggest, most confused frown I'd ever seen.

"He's your fiancé?"

"No he's not." I said.

"She is, I asked her yesterday," said Edward.

"I didn't say yes."

"You didn't say no."

I shrugged my shoulders.

"It wasn't even a proposal you crazy bastard it was a statement."

We were still screaming at each other when the cops arrived. I must say they were a lot quicker than their UK counterparts and quite physical too as they wrestled Edward into the back of one of their squad cars. They appeared to be quite friendly with François which worried me a little and the last thing I can recall was seeing Edward's doleful eyes as he looked out of the back of the car while they sped away and it broke my heart because I knew I could have stopped it.

After a few hours I insisted François call the police station and check if Edward was okay. François was confused and kept asking me if he was my fiancé or if I had any feelings for him. I couldn't lie; I reminded him that we'd had a relationship which I broke off when I caught him cheating. François seemed quite pleased at that admission and hugged me as he said he would never cheat on me as long as I lived. It was all very nice and pleasant and of course dinner followed later that evening at one of LA's finest and as I drank more and more champagne and grew drunker and drunker I found myself agreeing to everything François suggested including a holiday in Hawaii and extending my airline ticket by six months.

I woke up with the hangover from hell. I woke up in François' bed as naked as the day I was born and couldn't even remember leaving the restaurant. Oh My God I felt sick!

This was getting crazier by the second and it was spinning out of control. Poor Edward had spent the night in an LA police cell and I'd done God knows what with my one-time 'client' that I had gotten to seek professional help.

It was the most awful breakfast I'd ever had as François placed fruit and pastries and scrambled eggs in front of me and for the life of me I don't know how I didn't throw up. I tried a little fruit but as soon as the first tiny morsel hit my stomach I knew I would be seeing it again soon. The coffee was good though, the caffeine kicking in immediately. Oh shit! What had happened – what had I said and what had I done?

François must have been reading my mind.

"Don't worry," he said, "we didn't have sex."

"We didn't?"

"No."

"Then why are you looking so pleased with yourself?" I said.

And he was looking pleased, he almost looked smug, like the cat that got the cream.

"Because my darling, I've just spent the night sleeping in the same bed as the most beautiful girl in the world."

I reached for my coffee cup and took a long drink because I could tell François wasn't finished, it was almost as if he was about to deliver a lecture to a class of students.

"I've climbed the biggest mountain of my life Jessica, and it's all thanks to you."

"But we didn't have sex."

"No," he said, "but I've slept in a bed with a woman the whole night and that's the first time that's ever happened."

"You're winding me up?"

"I'm not Jessica, even my cousins kicked me out of their beds once they were finished with me, it's never happened before, it was beautiful just listening to you breathing and I feel on top of the world."

I was speechless... nearly.

"You mean...?"

"I'm ready for this Jessica; I've never been more ready for anything in my life. I'm ready for my therapist and I'm ready to settle down and make this work, I'm ready to consider spending the rest of my days with you."

With that he leaned forward and kissed me again and my head started spinning out of control.

I was lying on the floor when I regained consciousness. François was cradling my head in his arms as he held a cold cloth to my brow.

He looked relieved as he spoke.

"Thank God, thank God you're okay."

There was blood on his white robe.

"It's okay, it's nothing," he said. "You bumped your head on the table as you slipped off the chair. Speak to me Jessica, say something."

I reached up and stroked at the side of his face.

"What is it?" he said.

"Edward," I said, "we've got to get him out of there."

Chapter Twenty

I left one hell of a mess in LA when I jumped on the next plane after I knew Edward was safe and sound. I'd dropped all of the charges and I'd persuaded François to do the same. It wasn't difficult. He was angry at first, but then he was my 'cuck' and it took me no more than ten minutes to dominate him again and then he was eating out of the palm of my hand.

He would never change would poor François, despite the therapists and the counselling sessions and I knew it. Once a cuck, always a cuck, it was kind of engrained within him and who was I kidding to think I could change a man whose life had been shaped since childhood by an abusive family? I felt incredibly guilty walking out on him. Perhaps my heart wasn't in it; perhaps I didn't love him enough to give it a serious go and yet he sincerely believed he'd made giant strides forward in those few weeks we'd been together and I suppose in a way he had.

I needed time away from them both. It was just me and Russell again, like it used to be, like it always had been and as I lay tucked up in my bed watching TV with a half bottle of chardonnay and a shit DVD I felt secure and comfortable. Yet why did I feel as shit as the film I was watching.

I couldn't concentrate on it. Every two or three minutes I was thinking back to my time in LA and wondering if I could and should have done anything different. I felt guilty for the mess and destruction I had left behind, I felt like a tornado tearing through a small town ripping apart anything in its path. Edward had thought getting rescued from the cells had been my way of demonstrating that I had forgiven him and that we were an item again. The three of us had walked out of the police station together; to say the atmosphere was strained was an understatement as the two men bickered and argued all the way to the car and at one point I thought they were going to come to blows.

François drove back to Edward's hotel and we agreed that a 'clear the air session' was needed, so we headed for the hotel bar. Big mistake, but an even bigger mistake was that someone (I don't know who) ordered alcohol for me and as the first drink slipped down quite nicely, my headache miraculously disappeared and I quite naturally thought another drink was in order. Vodka and Redbull... another mistake, because now I was beginning to slip into the confident zone again and with the energy levels of a hungry lioness.

A drinker's world is a crazy place to be in. If something bad happens you drink to forget and if something good happens you drink to celebrate. Had something bad happened? I wasn't really sure. Had something good happened? Well yes, I suppose it had, at least we'd got Edward out of trouble so I suppose we were celebrating in a way.

Still they argued. Edward was prattling on about taking me back home to London and François was saying that I'd agreed to stay for another six months. It was bizarre, two grown men almost fighting over me and yet not one of them even bothered to consult me for my opinion.

After my fourth Vodka and Red Bull I excused myself and said I needed to go to the bathroom. I walked out of the bar, through the foyer of the hotel and jumped into a taxi which took me straight to François' house. The first text came in within about fifteen minutes. It was from François, wondering where I was. I texted back and said I felt like a lie down so I'd asked for Edward's room key from reception and he bought it.

The two of them would argue for another few hours and then they'd check my story out with reception and discover the subterfuge. By that time I would be at LAX airport with Russell, awaiting my flight back home.

The pilot announced we were flying over Chicago when I switched on my phone. Messages from François and messages from Edward, each declaring their undying love for me and begging to know that I was safe and sound and where I was.

I texted back 'somewhere over Chicago' and then switched my phone off and slept all the way to London.

I had sent a text to them both from the taxi en route back home. It was blunt and to the point, it read the same for both François and Edward. I said I needed space and time, I said the problem lay with me and that I was sorry but wasn't ready to settle down and have any man planning my life for me. I had said on no account was either of them to contact me until I had sorted myself out.

I returned to what I knew best and that was my business. It was surprisingly easy to pick it up again and towards the end of the week I had my first real time session, a regular client who took me to lunch while I ostracised and belittled him and thereafter maxed out his card on the high street.

By way of a small celebration I made him buy me a bottle of Cristal and as I bid him farewell phoned in a takeaway order to my favourite sushi restaurant. Everything was alright with the world as I snuggled up with Russell on the sofa and popped the cork on the champagne. I poured a glass and as I brought it towards my lips the doorbell rang.

"argghhhh!" I yelled out

I thought about not answering it but something pulled me towards the door. Before I even opened it I knew it was him and as I cast my eyes over the man who wouldn't take no for an answer I knew at that precise moment I loved him with all my heart and that I did indeed want to grow old with him.

"Jess, I'm sorry... I know you said..."

Before he could say another word I threw my arms around him and smothered him with kisses.

"The past is the past," I said. "Forget what's gone before, we all have our crosses to bear."

"But in LA when you ran out on me I thought it was over and I couldn't bear the thought of life without you. I was almost suicidal Jess."

I kissed him again.

"I understand now, I really do. I read up on the condition, it's been well researched and there are hundreds of sites on the internet and I know it's not your fault but we can work this out together."

A half smile pulled across his face as he realised I wasn't going to turn my back on him again. I told him I was so sorry for what I'd put him through and if there was anything I could do to make it up to him, he'd only to ask.

He looked nervous but he smiled.

"I'm sure I can think of something." he said.

Lightning Source UK Ltd.
Milton Keynes UK
UKOW04f1504040116

265735UK00001B/37/P